Modern Reader on the
Chinese Classics of
FLOWER ARRANGEMENT

On Vase Flower Arrangement
&
History of Vases

Modern Reader on the Chinese Classics of
FLOWER ARRANGEMENT

On Vase Flower Arrangement & History of Vases

By Zhang Qiande & Yuan Hongdao
Compiled by Li Xia

Better Link Press

This book is edited and designed by the Editorial Committee of *Cultural China* series.

Text by Zhang Qiande, Yuan Hongdao and Li Xia
Translation by Shelly Bryant
Cover Design by Wang Wei
Interior Design by Li Jing and Hu Bin (Yuan Yinchang Design Studio)

Copy Editor: Yang Xiaohe
Editors: Wu Yuezhou, Cao Yue
Editorial Director: Zhang Yicong

Senior Consultants: Sun Yong, Wu Ying, Yang Xinci
Managing Director and Publisher: Wang Youbu

ISBN: 978-1-60220-035-7

Address any comments about *Modern Reader on the Chinese Classics of Flower Arrangement: On Vase Flower Arrangement & History of Vases* to:

Better Link Press
99 Park Ave
New York, NY 10016
USA

or

Shanghai Press and Publishing Development Co., Ltd.
F 7 Donghu Road, Shanghai, China (200031)
Email: comments_betterlinkpress@hotmail.com

Printed in China by Shenzhen Donnelley Printing Co., Ltd.

1 3 5 7 9 10 8 6 4 2

Quanjing provides the images on pages 54, 57–61, 63 and 68.
Plant Photo Bank of China (PPBC) provides the images on pages 52–54, 57, 59, 62–70 and 106–107.

Fig. 3 *Spring at the Palace*
(detail)

Qiu Ying (c. 1505–c. 1551)
Ink and color on silk
Height 34.2 cm × Width 474.5 cm
Palace Museum, Taibei

This painting depicts the daily choreography of early spring at the palace: makeup, watering plants, pruning branches, flower arrangement, feeding, singing and dancing, playing instruments, dining at a family reunion, playing chess, reading, playing with the grass, looking in the mirror, observing painting, children at play, offering food, and swaying fans. The painting which includes the concubines, palace maids, princes, eunuchs, and painters, 115 in all, fully displays the artist's superb skills.

On page 1
Fig. 1 *Enjoying Plum Blossom*
(detail)
Please refer to page 22.

On pages 2 and 3
Fig. 2 *One Hundred Flowers*
(detail)
Please refer to pages 42 and 43.

CONTENTS

露山玄蓮供觀畫一于
深柳讀書堂

FOREWORD

Vase flower arrangement, originating perhaps with the offering of flowers before the Buddha in the Eastern Han Dynasty (25–220) and the Wei and Jin dynasties (220–420), expanded through the Tang (618–907) and Song (960–1279) dynasties to become quite popular. In the Song Dynasty what was most popular were *qinggong* (fig. 4), decorations placed on a desk in the main hall or in the study to create ambience, such as vase flowers, seasonal fruits, rockeries, antiques, and the scholar's four treasures. At that time, the vase flowers became an important part of the daily life of the literati in China. This volume includes two books produced in the Ming Dynasty (1368–1644), *On Vase Flower Arrangement* (*Pinghua Pu*) by Zhang Qiande (1577–1643) and *History of Vases* (*Ping Shi*) by Yuan Hongdao (1568–1610). Written in 1595 and 1599, these are the earliest monographs detailing the theory of vase flower arrangement, and are often referred to as two classical treasures on China's floral arts.

Fig. 4 *Decoration for Appreciation*
Chen Hongshou (1598–1652)

The decoration on the desk of the ancient Chinese scholar for appreciation expresses the master's artistic taste and philosophical ideal. Chen Hongshou's painting, with distinctive classical traits, represents the classic style of the late Ming Dynasty. The sophisticated taste presented in the only existing plain-style decoration in the painting, with the maple leaves symbolizing the passing ages, was widely recognized by the scholars at that time.

1. Historical Background

Theoretical works on China's elegant art forms frequently appeared during this particular period in history. To understand this phenomenon, we must start with a look at the historical background. At that time, China was at a turning point in which the Ming court flourished and the bureaucratic ranks swelled with various affiliations and rivalries. There was a great deal of corruption in the government, and the imperial exams did not go smoothly; there was constant unrest and great trials, with difficulties pressing in both internally and externally, putting a great strain on the government and the people. At the same time, the handicraft and commodity economy flourished in the Ming Dynasty, and a commercial market and capitalism were sprouting, surpassing any dynasty before it.

The Jiangnan area was situated some distance from the capital. It was not a political center, but had beautiful scenery and an affluent economy. The traditional literati class was freed from the traditional concept of "literature expressing political ideals," leaving them instead free to seek for a slow-paced art-oriented life and to express their own personalities and emotions. As a result, Jiangnan culture brought about a cultured assembly, providing a solid foundation for the literati class. Most members of this class lived in secluded private gardens, where they lived elegant lifestyles and produced elegant art, holding numerous banquets and other amusements, composing poetry and music, communing with nature, and pursuing

Fig. 5 *A Painting of Elegant Gathering at the West Garden*

Qiu Ying
Ink and color on silk
Height 141 cm × Width 66.3 cm
Palace Museum, Taibei

It has been said that the gathering of Su Shi (1037–1101), Huang Tingjian (1045–1105), Qin Guan (1049–1100), and other scholars at the West Garden during the Song Dynasty was a major event in the literary community, based on which Qiu Ying drew this picture to depict the ideal venue for a meeting of men of letters in that time. Amid the mountainous forest, with exquisite pavilions and terraces, bamboos, rockeries and flowers, accompanied by concubines and boy attendants, and surrounded by friends and scholars, one would ask for no greater bliss on earth.

Ming Dynasty Celebrities and the Garden

The Ming Dynasty scholar Wang Shizhen (1526–1590) hailed from the Wang family in Taicang, a household generations of noblemen. His father was Wang Yu (1507–1560), the Left Vice Minister of the Ministry of War. The elder Wang had superb abilities, but offended Yan Song (1480–1567) and his son, and after a defeat suffered in the Luan He War, he was thrown in prison. Wang Shizhen and his brother Wang Shimao (1536–1588) pleaded with the house of Yan on their father's behalf. Yan Song made a false display of sympathy, but was in fact utterly ruthless. In 1560, Wang Yu, a great cultured officer who "managed the border issues at an old age and was dedicated to the country," was beheaded in an extremely cruel act. Wang Shizhen and his brother wept bitterly as they escorted the deceased home for funerary rites. Learning from his brutish career, Wang Shizhen retreated to his home and built Yanshan Garden, which covered a space of more than 70 *mu* (roughly 46, 500 m^2). He built numerous pavilions and galleries, and planted all the best trees and shrubs. As a leader of the Jiangnan literary world, Wang Shizhen saw many more ups and downs in his life of officialdom, but he always credited the garden as his source of energy.

Some people did not want to be officials, even if not confronted with setbacks. One example was An Shaofang (Ming Dynasty) from Wuxi, Jiangsu Province.

An Shaofang's great grandfather, An Guo, built a garden with a pool in it. It was not a large garden, but one year when a drought affected many people in the area around Wuxi, An dug more waterways to help provide relief. The victims of the drought flocked to the garden, where An fed nearly a thousand people each day. After the meal had been eaten, the entire contingent set to work digging more ponds. With the collective strength of such great numbers, they soon dug up hundreds of *mu* of waterways, and before long, the land had again offered its rich produce.

An Shaofang inherited the family tradition of gardening. Having been born to a genteel family, he was considered quite a promising young fellow, but without any hesitation, he gave up bright career prospects to go home and care for the family garden. Later, his brother-in-law, Qin Yao, became frustrated with his own life in officialdom. An promptly encouraged him to return home and build a garden, too, which is now known as Jichang Garden in Wuxi.

Many similar anecdotes exist that give us a glimpse of the wonders associated with the secluded life of a garden.

lofty ideals. According to the records of that time, when the literati "read classic books, practiced calligraphy and meditation, talked with friends over wine, watered flowers and grew bamboos, listened to music and raised birds, burnt incense and made tea, climbed up the city walls to see mountains, and played chess," they considered the leisurely, delicate lives they lived a matter of fact to be taken in their stride (fig. 5).

The gardens in which the members of the literati class lived were beautiful and picturesque, so the furnishings of the living quarters, the decorations on the tables, the utensils in the studies, the objects of amusement, and the garden architecture all became points of interest for the literati. As a result, many books were written to describe the lifestyle of the literati, including works such as *Treatise on Superfluous Things* (*Zhangwu Zhi*), *The Book of Excerpts* (*Zunsheng Bajian*), *On Antiques for Appreciation* (*Kaopan Yushi*), *On Vase Flower Arrangement*, and *History of Vases*. These works were written to provide an authoritative reference to the elegant lifestyle of the literati.

2. Why Attention Is Given to Flower Vases

If we say that floral vase arrangements originated with the flower offerings before the Buddha in the Wei and Jin dynasties, we can see a line of development through the palace decorations of the Tang-Song periods to the place of respect such arrangements gained among the literati during the late Ming Dynasty. At this point, vase floral arrangements became well loved, coupling the values of companionship and seclusion.

In *Record of a Small Window* (*Xiaochuang Youji*), Ming Dynasty writer and calligrapher Chen Jiru (1558–1639) records, "Flowers are arranged in a vase, and rockeries in a pot. Although such an arrangement is quite conventional, these pieces are always full of personality and extremely interesting. How can each arrangement be so full of vitality?" From this passage, we see that vase and flower arrangements were so highly valued at that time because the literati linked the vase to the nature of a scholar, and so sought to shape the scholar's daily life through placement of such objects that represented desirable values. In the portraits depicted by the late Ming painter Chen Hongshou, wherever a gentleman is represented, he is bound to be accompanied by a vase, usually holding flowers, such as the lotus, chrysanthemum, or winding twigs of plum blossom, in very lively images (figs. 6–7).

Fig. 7 *Playing Music with the Company of Wine and Poetry*
Chen Hongshou
Ink and color on paper
Height 168 cm × Width 84 cm

Chen Hongshou, skillful in presenting his reclusive life, depicted in this picture Lao Lian (Chen himself) drinking wine with his close friend, with a maid standing by with the musical instrument, a picture of harmony and serenity. With a preference for big and tall vases in the painting, Chen depicted the old servant holding a huge vase, though merely its upper part was revealed.

Fig. 6 *Drinking Tea* (detail)
Chen Hongshou
Ink and color on silk
Height 75 cm × Width 53 cm
Duoyunxuan Collection

The painting depicts two officials, seated facing one another as they drink tea. The host sits on a plantain leaf, holding a teacup in hand. His guest sits on a large rock. A huge bronze vase is next to him, holding two brightly colored lotus flowers.

Fig. 8 *"Bamboo Shelter for Antiques"* **from the**
Figure Story Album

Qiu Ying
Ink and color on silk
Height 41.4 cm × Width 33.8 cm
Palace Museum, Beijing

This painting depicts antique appreciation in a garden. The literati are gathered in the bamboo shelter, appreciating ancient calligraphies and paintings. The table is full of large bronze pieces, ancient and mottled with rust. They are exaggeratedly decorative. A bronze *gu* is placed below, acting as a vase. It holds a bright piece of red coral.

3. Zhang Qiande and *On Vase Flower Arrangement*

In discussing late Ming reclusive scholars from Jiangnan, Zhang Qiande is undoubtedly one of the key figures. One of the most important painting and calligraphy connoisseurs, collectors and cataloguer, Zhang penned the text *On Vase Flower Arrangement*. His own name was Qiande, but at the age of ten, he was given the name Chou, and was thus later called Zhang Chou. Other aliases included the pen name Guangde, along with Qing Fu, Qing Pu, Qinghe Niulang, and late in life, Mi An, with his studies named Zhengjin Zhai, Baomi Xuan, and so forth.

Zhang Qiande grew up as a child meticulously nurtured in a prestigious family. The Zhang family was prominent in Kunshan, an area of Jiangnan. His grandfather, Zhang Qing, was given the official post during the Jiajing period (1522–1566) of the Ming Dynasty, serving in the Nanjing Ministry of War. Zhang Qiande's great uncle, Zhang Yi, also sat for the imperial exams and worked for the Ministry of Works. However, after failing the exam on several occasions, Zhang Qiande's father, Zhang Yingwen eventually gave up trying to pass, instead retiring to a life of leisure, painting and writing calligraphies. His writings and calligraphies, along with his rich collection of books, indicate a life of learning and are an exemplary of good quality works.

The Zhang family had an air of culture and learning about them, and they owned an elegant collection of books. In his preface to *Qinghe Paintings and Calligraphies* (*Qinghe Shuhua Fang*), Zhang Qiande says, "There was a time when my family collections of paintings and calligraphies was the finest in the Zhongwu area." The paintings and books collected by the Zhang family included many world-renowned treasures, such as the Western Jin Dynasty (265–316) writer Lu Ji's (261–303) calligraphy *Ping Fu Tie*, Eastern Jin Dynasty (317–420) calligrapher Wang Xizhi's (321–379, or, 303–361, or, 307–365) work *Er Xie Tie*, Eastern Jin Dynasty calligrapher Wang Xianzhi's (344–386) work *Mid-Autumn Festival*, Tang Dynasty calligrapher Yan Zhenqing's (708–784) piece *Liu Zhongshi*, Yuan Dynasty (1279–1368) painter and calligrapher Zhao Mengfu's (1254–1322) painting *Three Mountains in Autumn*, and Northern Song Dynasty (960–1127) emperor, painter and calligrapher Huizong's (1082–1135) painting *Plum and Cuckoo*. From the directory of such a collection, the wealth of possessions and financial strength of the Zhang household is apparent. The family was closely linked to the circle of old writers in the Wuzhong area, and Zhang Yingwen and Wang Shizhen were inextricably connected. The story of the Zhang household is not just a family history, but a tale of the cultural elites in the region (fig. 8).

On Vase Flower Arrangement was compiled in 1595. It was one of China's earliest monograph on the art of vase and flower arrangements. The book is divided into eight sections: Appreciating Vases, Picking Flowers, Floral Arrangement, Cultivation, Related Matters, Taboos, and Vase Maintenance. The first two sections are more detailed. The book is a true classic of Ming Dynasty floral art, elaborating on the natural spirit of freestyle floral arrangements, advocating a natural feel along with the pursuit of one's innate natural interests.

Zhang Qiande's neat style provides a concise, fresh perspective on the matter, straight to the point and without concerns over irrelevant issues. Fortunately, he did not have to spend his time governing as part of the Ming court, but was instead left to spend his leisurely life living in peace and dignity.

Fig. 9 *Inscribing Verses about Bamboo*

Du Jin (Ming Dynasty)
Ink and color on silk
Height 189.5 cm × Width 104 cm
Palace Museum, Beijing

Yuan Hongdao prefers to use bamboo. Bamboo is representative of a gentleman, and since ancient times has been taken as a symbol of a nobleman. This painting depicts the story of Su Shi's inscribing verses about bamboo. Bamboo is depicted as vigorous and strong, with branches and leaves nicely laid-out and balanced in color, which highlights the excellent, clean brushwork.

4. Yuan Hongdao and *History of Vases*

Yuan Hongdao, who became an official during the Wanli period (1573–1620) of the Ming Dynasty, was the author of *History of Vases*. He was named magistrate in Wuxian County, and also served as an official in Beijing, even becoming Director of the Ministry of Personnel. He was a well-known writer whose works were fresh, clear, and straightforward. His essays were highly praised for promoting a literary spirit and originality. Yuan Hongdao was fond of traveling, and he possessed great knowledge. Though he always remained detached from political affairs, he had a wealth of social experience and was well-versed in the affairs of the world.

History of Vases was compiled in 1599, four years after *On Vase Flower Arrangement*. *History of Vases* is divided into twelve sections: Categories of Flowers, Grades, Vessels, Selecting Water, Propriety, Eschewing Worldliness, Hindrances to Flower Cultivation, Bathing, Flowers as Foils, Amateurish Attachment, Appreciation, and Supervision. From these chapters, we learn a great deal about flower selection and the art of flower arrangement.

It is worth noting that Yuan Hongdao applied his literary theory of "spirituality and spiritualism" to flower arrangement, giving a deeper meaning to the horticultural arts (fig. 9). For this reason, *History of Vases* spread to Japan, where it became very popular. The Japanese people think of Yuan Hongdao as a greatly cultured writer, and they take great inspiration from his elaborations on the art of floral arrangements.

5. Comparing *On Vase Flower Arrangement* and *History of Vases*

Because both of these volumes are focused on flower arrangement (fig. 10), there is no lack

Fig. 10 *Decoration for Appreciation on the First Day of the Lunar Calendar*
Wu Guichen (Qing Dynasty, 1644–1911)
Ink and color on paper
Height 112 cm × Width 54 cm
In this painting, a blue glazed vase holds plum blossoms, peony, and camellia. In a wicker basket are fresh peaches, a cutting of white plum, and several fronds of grass. It is a simple painting with a folk feel.

of similarity between the text and perspectives in the two books. However, each has its own strengths and weaknesses.

The primary difference lies in the very different backgrounds of the two authors. Zhang Qiande was renowned for his collection of paintings and calligraphies. He was the author of the twelve scrolls comprising *Qinghe Paintings and Calligraphies*, in which he recorded and circulated

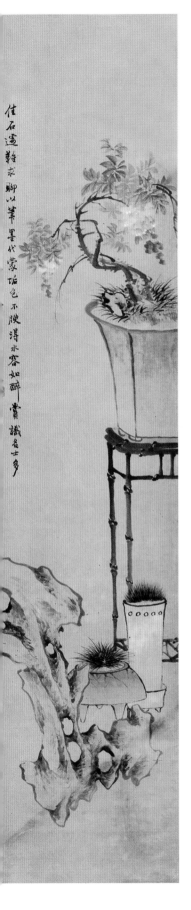

numerous famous paintings and calligraphies. The record ranges from the earliest, Zhong Yao (151–230) of the Three Kingdoms Period (220-280) to the latest, a Ming Dynasty piece by Qiu Ying, including a total of 140 writers, 49 texts, and 150 paintings. He also made extensive notes on the lives of many authors. Because it is so systematic, the book is rich in content, citing numerous references. For a long time, it has been the main reference point for connoisseurs seeking to prove the authenticity of a particular work,

Fig. 11 *Decoration for Appreciation on Four Screens*

Mu Zhong (Qing Dynasty)
Ink and color on paper
Height 130 cm × Width 30 cm × 4

Mu Zhong was from Jiaxing, in today's Zhejiang Province. He was skilled at sketching or drawing from life (*xiesheng*).

and has thus been very influential. However, Yuan Hongdao was a typical member of the literati class and a representative of the Ming Dynasty Gong'an School. He advocated "expressing independence of soul without being confined to conventions, and refusing to put down what are not one's true and original feelings and thoughts."

In addition, the choice of flowers covered in the two works is quite different. Yuan Hongdao advocates a rigid adherence to selection of particular types of flowers, such as the peony, plum blossom, or chrysanthemum (fig. 11). He is quite conservative, lacking novelty in his ideas. Zhang Qiande, on the other hand, could create great wonder out of mundane items, and had great insight into all sorts of plants and flowers. He occasionally even used some uncommon flowers, such as symplocos, lophatherum, citrus uranium, or lesser galangal. There was no end to his use of such flowers, and he exhausted every means of exploration. He possessed the so-called "daring of the artist," and his great vision and ability in arrangement made him bold in his choice of flowers. Those who lack skill in arrangement tend to make more conservative flower selections.

Finally the styles of the two books are different. Zhang Qiande concentrates on specific matters in plain, straightforward language, without adding much meaning beyond what is evident on the surface. Yuan Hongdao, on the other hand, has given us a carefully crafted text with many asides and numerous anecdotes, unconfirmed legends, marketplace fashions, and all sorts of similar notes. In discussing horticultural arts, Yuan Hongdao offers a deeper examination than Zhang Qiande, most likely arising from his superior skills in both analytical thought and writing. He manages to express these complex ideas in plain language, creating a smooth, very readable text that captures the imagination.

6. Artistic Style in Ming Dynasty Flower Arrangement

The genteel classes of the Ming Dynasty literati held flower arrangement in great esteem and gave great attention to natural beauty. In their view, whether vase flowers were expansive and flexible, light and charming, or quaint and heavy, they had to have a sense of naturalness. Aiming at exquisite and graceful, they did not have to pursue a neat, symmetrical sense of ritual (fig. 12).

It was almost universal among reclusive characters to have an aversion to order. If such people had been drawn to stylized or ritualistic things, they would not have lived in seclusion, evading secular interaction (figs. 13–14). Vase flower arrangements were one example of things suited to solitude, suited to expressing the independent, unconventional spirit.

Several well-known Ming Dynasty practitioners of vase flower art, such as Zhang Qiande, Wen Zhenheng (1585–1645), and Chen Hongshou, were also calligraphers and painters. Wen Zhenheng was a great painter, continuing the family tradition of art, following his great grandfather Wen Zhengming (1470–1559). As noted above, Zhang Qiande was a noted collector of calligraphies and paintings. Chen Hongshou himself was a renowned artist. A less cultured person would find it hard to progress very far along the path to great art. Conversely, for

Fig. 12 *Decoration for Appreciation on the First Day of the Lunar*

Ma Quan (Qing Dynasty)
Ink and color on paper
Height 93 cm × Width 32 cm

Ma Quan, a female painter in the mid-Qing Dynasty from Changshu, Jiangsu Province, was a noble and elegant artist, as is revealed in the refined style of this painting. In the ceramic vase were plum blossoms and a single peony, plain and refined; the daffodils in the basin, the finger citrons on the plate and the persimmons on the floor were all commonly seen flowers for appreciation during the Qing Dynasty.

those who did manage to get onto that road, it became relatively easy to travel far along it. Whether considering Zhang Qiande or Yuan Hongdao, it is worth noting that, for them, flower arranging was merely a hobby, and yet they managed to engage in it at such a professional level, allowing their texts to become high points among the classics in the history of flower arrangement. This is a sort of skill that extends well beyond the art itself.

Li Xia

Figs. 13–14 *A Dwelling amid Bamboos in the Mountain*
Shen Zhen (Ming Dynasty)
Ink and color on paper
Height 115.5 cm × Width 35 cm
Liaoning Provincial Museum

Shen Zhen, born in the second year of the Jianwen period (1400), was the uncle of Shen Zhou (1427–1509), a master painting artist in the Ming Dynasty. In the picture a clear river winded its way across the mountains, dotted with trees, pavilions and a dwelling where a monk and a man were sitting opposite to each other, chatting at a table with a vase of flowers on it. Outside the house a novice monk was making tea beside the bamboos while another man was following the path into the depths of the mountain. The picture depicts a delicate delight in tranquility.

ON VASE FLOWER ARRANGEMENT

By Zhang Qiande (Ming Dynasty)

Fig. 16 *Enjoying Plum Blossom*

Chen Hongshou
Ink and color on silk
Height 83 cm × Width
43.5 cm

White plum, dark pots, and the expression of the host and guest focused on admiring the plum form the focal point at the visual center of the picture. The figure touches the plum blossom with a finger, seeming to instruct the attentive guests in the art of flower appreciation. The flower containers in the picture include a flat round black porcelain vase, holding a single stalk of plum blossom, demonstrating a clear, elegant, solitary style.

PREFACE

THE ORIGINAL TEXT

The scholar who dreamt of the butterfly said: When you take refuge in a world of solitude, you might find it hard to comprehend the essence of a vase of flowers. There are few people who are familiar with it. In looking back, it is clear Jin Run was able to write *On Vase and Flower Arrangement* at a young age. I wrote these articles when I was just eighteen. Which of them are right or wrong and how to choose between them is for one who can comprehend and naturally judges fairly. I will not say more than that. Written two days before Mid-Autumn Festival, 1595.

THE MODERN READER

"The scholar who dreamt of the butterfly" is the name by which Zhang Qiande called himself. The allusion is from the story of "Zhuangzi Dreams of the Butterfly," and is Zhang's way of honoring Laozi (Spring and Autumn Period, 770–476 BC) and Zhuangzi (c. 369–c. 286 BC) and their thought. Perhaps influenced in this regard by his father, Zhang Qiande had already aspired to live a secluded life. When he wrote this, he was just eighteen years old, and he acknowledged his youth.

The article mentions Jin Run (b. 1405), a Ming Dynasty scholar and painter from Shangyuan (now Nanjing), Jiangsu Province. He was diligent in study early in his childhood, then at the age of twelve, began composing poetry. He excelled at rhyming, painting, and calligraphy. His landscape paintings are clean, neat, and display rigorous attention to composition, with balanced density. It is said that he composed a book entitled *On Vase Flower Arrangement* early on, but that text has been lost.

The literati who lived in the splendid region of Jiangnan believed the vase flower arrangement was an essential skill to be nurtured by the cultured class. The accumulation of cultural heritage among the people of Jiangnan was not something that arose quickly, but was instead the result of several generations of devoted scholarship. It is precisely because of this that Zhang Qiande was able to arrange vase flowers when he was young, and he used the virtues learned through the practice of this art as a basis for addressing his readers (fig. 16).

On pages 20 and 21
Fig. 15 *Antique Appreciation* (detail)
Du Jin
Ink and color on silk
Height 126.1 cm × Width 187 cm
Palace Museum, Taibei
The painting depicts two scholars dedicated to appreciating the antiquities on a long table, vividly reflecting the leisurely enjoyment of ancient artefacts common among the mid and late Ming Dynasty literati class.

CHAPTER 1
APPRECIATING VASES

THE ORIGINAL TEXT

The first task involved in flower arrangement is choosing a vase. As a general rule, bronzeware is a better fit for spring and winter, while porcelain is suited for autumn and summer, varying materials with the change of seasons. Large vases are made for halls of splendor and grandeur (fig. 17), while smaller vases are more ideal for studies, varying the vase's size according to its placement. Of materials used in crafting vases, porcelain and bronze are valued more than gold and silver for their purity and elegance. Ring ears on a vase and vases displayed in pairs are always in poor taste, as this calls to mind temples and sacrifices. The opening of the vase should be small and the base thick, allowing it to sit steadily and keep its essence contained inside.

In most cases, a thin vase is favored over a plump one, and a small one over a large one. A vase should not be more than one

Fig. 17 *A Collection of Auspice*
Giuseppe Castiglione (1688–1766)
Ink and color on silk
Height 173 cm × Width 86.1 cm
Palace Museum, Taibei

Depicted in the painting is a blue porcelain vase with bowstring pattern, in which twin lotuses, seedpods, and ears of rice are presented, pointing to good fortune. Giuseppe Castiglione was an Italian missionary to China during the 54th year of the Qing Emperor Kangxi's reign (1715), and he later entered the Palace's Ruyi Museum. He painted in China for more than 50 years, greatly influencing the aesthetic tastes of Qing Court paintings after Kangxi (1654–1722).

chi (approximately 31.3 cm) tall, with six to seven *cun* (roughly 18.66 to 21.77 cm) or four to five *cun* (roughly 12.44 to 15.55 cm) vases being most preferred. If a vase is too small, the flowers it holds will not survive for long.

The bronzeware suitable for arranging flowers include *zun* (a wine vessel), *lei* (an urn-shaped wine vessel), *gu* (a drinking vessel), and a pot, all of which were used to hold wine in ancient times, but now seem quite appropriate to contain flowers.

Ancient bronze bottles and bowls, buried underground for ages and immersed in soil, are perfect for growing flowers, which bloom in bright colors as if on branches, blossoming early and withering slowly. In some cases, when flowers wither, they may bear fruit in the vessel. Ancient bronzeware such as *shuixiu* (water scale or encrusted) and *chuanshigu* (which looks like bright black paint as a result of oxidation) are cases in point. The same is true of pottery buried underground for thousands of years.

In ancient times, there were no porcelain bottles, so copper ones were used instead. It was not until the Tang Dynasty that porcelain products from distinguished kilns were highly valued. Since the Tang Dynasty, renowned kilns such as Chai, Ru, Ge, Ding, Longquan, Jun, Zhangsheng, Wuni, Xuande, and Chenghua emerged, producing a variety of earthenware. For the presentation of elegance, nothing tops bronzeware, but among porcelain ware, the most precious

Fig. 18 *Listening to the Qin (Zither) in the Courtyard*
Du Jin
Ink and color on silk
Height 163 cm × Width 94.5 cm

This painting presents the daily life of a man of letters in the Ming Dynasty, who played the zither in the courtyard, with a lady listening attentively behind a screen. A plain rattan bed with books and paintings for daily reading was where a scholar studied. There is a vase of blooming flowers on the table beside the rockeries from Taihu (Lake Tai), under the plantain. On the zither table there is another small, thin vase, for just one or two flowers.

pieces are from Chai and Ru kilns, which are now extinct. Those from Guan, Ge, Xuande, and Ding kilns are today's top treasures, and bottles from Longquan, Jun, Zhangsheng, Wuni, and Chenghua kilns are precious, ranking in the order listed.

For various ancient pots, gallbladder-shaped vases, *zun*, *gu*, and vases for a single flower, porcelain agrees perfectly with both study and living area. Small yarrow bottles, paper-mallet bottles, plain round bottles, and goose-neck bottles can likewise be used for flower arrangement. In contrast, medicine jars such as *anhua*, eggplant bag bottles, gourd-shaped bottles, thin bottles with small openings, flat-belly bottles, and thin-bottom bottles are not suitable as table decoration for the study.

Among ancient bronze pots and porcelain bottles from the Longquan and Jun kilns, huge ones of up to two or three *chi* (roughly 62.6 to 93.9 cm) in height, are of little use, except in winter, when large branches of plum blossoms can be arranged with sulfur inside the vessel as table decoration.

THE MODERN READER

Horticultural arts prospered in the middle and late Ming Dynasty. In the homes of the gentry in Jiangnan, there were always spaces allotted for living, banqueting, reading, decorating, and so forth (fig. 18). The first task of flower arranging was the selection of flower vessels. The ancients referred to flower vessels as "the golden house of flowers" or "the house of flowers," and each flower had to be perfectly matched and deftly inserted into the vessel, creating a perfect blend of flowers in a unique floral design. People in the Ming Dynasty paid attention to the choices of vessels' materials, shapes, sizes and settings.

1. Decorations for Rituals and Decorations for Appreciation

Here, it is necessary to introduce two types of flower arrangements, decorations for rituals and decorations for appreciation.

The symbolic and etiquette functions of decorations for rituals made them a special sort of flower arrangement. It was usually placed in a magnificent hall during important occasions such as the Spring Festival, the Dragon Boat Festival, or the Mid-Autumn Festival. For this reason, this type of flower arrangement was grand, elegant, magnificent, and natural. The vase in which it was held was quite costly and glorious, making a perfect match. It was customary to offer a decoration for rituals during the Song Dynasty. During the Ming and Qing dynasties, it was more common to use many types of flowers with rich composition and images of prosperity (fig. 19).

Decorations for appreciation became popular in the Song Dynasty. This type of arrangement was meant to be placed on a desk for viewing in the main hall or study as

Fig. 19 *Vase Flowers* (detail)
With Cixi Inscription
Qing Dynasty

There are quite a number of pictures of vase flowers with Cixi's inscription, most of which are actually works of court painters. This picture features peonies, magnolias, crabapples, pomegranate blossoms and Chinese roses, with luxuriant twigs and blossoms, and an overall pattern that is magnificently elegant and plainly refined, revealing the unparalleled flowers cultivated at court.

an additional delight. There were two meanings associated with the term decorations for appreciation. One was reference to elegant items such as pine, bamboo, plum blossoms, and other plants, along with incense, seasonal fruits, and other light foods. The other referred to *penjing* (bonsai), rockeries, antiques, the four scholar's treasures, or other items for entertainment. The literati referred to decorations for appreciation as "a sacrifice," so only stylish, tasteful materials were to be used in its arrangement. The decorations for appreciation were divided into "named" and "unnamed." The "named" were to be used for festivals, such as the decorations for appreciation on the first day of the lunar calendar (fig. 20), decorations for appreciation on the Dragon Boat Festival (fig. 21), or decorations for appreciation on the Mid-Autumn Festival. They could also be assigned to certain occasions, such as decorations for appreciation at birthdays, weddings, or coming-of-age ceremonies. The "unnamed" arrangements were not assigned to particular times or festivals, but were

Fig. 20 *Decoration for Aappreciation on the First Day of the Lunar Calendar*
Yang Jin (Qing Dynasty)
Ink and color on paper
Height 82.5 cm × Width 29 cm

This painting is a typical model of flower arrangement in winter, in which there are no narcissus usually presented for refined appreciation on the first day of the lunar calendar, but instead, pine twigs (representing evergreen life in winter), wintersweet (representing delicate fragrance), nandina (representing the bright color of fruits). The three types of flowers' putting together forms a perfect match, blending color, fragrance, and fine quality.

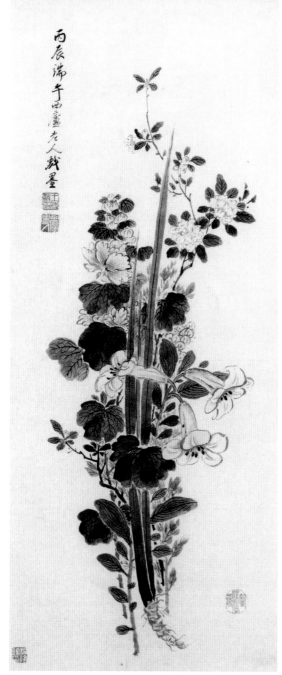

Fig. 21 *Dragon Boat Festival*
Wang Shimin (1592–1680)
Ink on paper
Height 100.8 cm × Width 40.1 cm
Palace Museum, Beijing

Wang Shimin, from Taicang, Jiangsu Province, crowned as a leader in the painting community early in the Qing Dynasty, was known for his landscape painting, with his style directly influencing many who came after. This picture was specially drawn for the Dragon Boat Festival, depicting calami, hollyhocks, hosta plantaginea, roses (rosa multiflora), and other early summer blossoms. It was customary to bind calami for the festival and the painting presents the auspicious, festive atmosphere.

used at any time one pleased for leisure and appreciation.

Flowers for rituals and flowers for appreciation were arranged differently. In a magnificent hall, a large vase with flowers, usually peonies, created an elegant atmosphere. Placed in a study, the literati felt a flower held great significance. In daily use, it was a symbolic of a liberal lifestyle, conveying the spirit of the literati. For such arrangements, the elegant gardenia or sweetly fragranced osmanthus was preferred, filling the entire room with the aroma so that all who entered would forget the world outside, and the overall style of the room would be made noble and elegant.

2. Size and Materials of the Flower Vessels

Flower vessels were chosen to suit their environment. For instance, flowers for rituals had to be magnificent, while flowers for a scholar's study had to pay more attention to smaller blossoms, since they were used in the smaller spaces of studies or living areas.

In regards to the study, Zhang Qiande believed that the vase should be slim, not too plump, and that one too small was preferable to one that was too large. Sharing this point of view, the Ming Dynasty dramatist Gao Lian (c. 1527–c. 1603), Ming Dynasty opera composer and writer Tu Long (1543–1605), and others followed Tu Long's principle of "the best types of vase should be gallipots and small square vases … for orchids or cymbidium, a drinking vessel (*hu*) should be used, or for peonies, a cattail mallet vase." The selection of flowers and the shape and size of the vases were to be considered. For instance, the peony was not suited to a small, thin vase. However, some people favored the use of tall, strong vases, such as Chen Hongshou, a nobleman and artist. His vase always held a wealth of flowers. For instance, in *Playing Music with the Company of Wine and Poetry* (see fig. 7 on page 11), the old servant holds a flower. Although only the upper part is exposed, it looks very strong.

In fact, the vase size mentioned by Zhang Qiande probably only applied to the vases from Song Dynasty kilns, which would not include the plum vase. Although the plum vase was popular since the Song Dynasty, it was plump, but quite tall, so did not meet the thin, slim aesthetic standard. We can see that the Zhang family usually placed their flower arrangements in treasures from particular kilns. Zhang Qiande was accustomed to seeing these, so that became his standard for flower arrangements. In fact, the size of Ming Dynasty flower arrangements were quite different from those of the Song Dynasty. Although thinness was judged beautiful, many were also stout and yet sill beautiful. One example was the plum vase, which during the Jiajing and Wanli periods of the Ming Dynasty was significantly higher than it had been in earlier times. Its body grew gradually larger, to the point that a plain tricolor vase with interlocking lotus design on a white ground was 63.4 cm. Tall, large vases abounded in the Qing Dynasty, such as the large glazed Qianlong period vases, which were up to 86 cm.

In terms of textiles, vases could be made of copper, pottery, porcelain, gold, silver, bamboo, wood, or other materials. The Ming literati class emphasized elegant beauty, so porcelain and bronze were preferred for vases, while gold and silver were taboo. Imagine a blooming plum blossom or a bunch of white chrysanthemum with a burst of surging fragrance. If inserted into a bronze bottle, this would be quite quaint. In porcelain, it would offer a noble sense of pleasure. In a yellowy golden vase, it would appear vulgar, and in a silver or tin vase, it would be particularly out of place, creating a sense of discord between flowers and vessel.

3. Bronzeware and Its Types

During the Shang and Zhou dynasties (1600–256 BC), bronzeware was the most important product in the country, and bronze items were considered noble and sublime. Such pieces have always been among the secret treasures of the imperial palace in China. As early as the Western Han Dynasty (206 BC–AD 25), bronzeware had become something emperors competed for, hoping to expand their collections. For this reason, bronzeware was easily obtainable by most people in the Ming Dynasty as vessels for vase flower arrangements. Most of these, though, were fakes. Of course, there were still many people who used authentic bronzeware vases for their arrangements.

It is evident that by the late Ming Dynasty, some concepts from the traditional ritual system were quite weak among the literati in Jiangnan. The use of bronzeware for vase flower arrangements was common in the Ming Dynasty, and was particularly useful for advocating "conversance with the ancient."

Of course, one very important reason for this phenomenon was that in the Ming Dynasty, a great number of imitation pre-Qin (i.e., before 221 BC) bronzeware pieces were produced, which resulted in the old items from the nobility "flying into the homes of ordinary people." Even ordinary scholars could afford them. The history of imitation pre-Qin bronzeware dates back to the Song Dynasty. In the Xuanhe period (1119–1125), on Huizong's orders, the Northern Song Dynasty minister Wang Fu compiled the *Study of the Ancient in the Xuanhe Period* (*Xuanhe Bogu Tu*), a record of the major bronzeware pieces collected by the Song Dynasty's imperial family. This formed the basic reference material used by later copyists. The Ming Dynasty continued the antique style of the Song Dynasty, and even expanded it. For instance, during the Xuande period (1426–1435), the fifth emperor of the Ming Dynasty, the Emperor Xuangzong,

Bronzeware Suitable for Flower Arrangement

Zhang Qiande believed that the vessels, jars, pots, and bowls used to hold wine were suitable for containing flowers.

Zun (尊): During the Shang and Zhou dynasties, this type of vessel was for ritual use and for holding wine. It has ring foot, with a round or square belly, long neck, and open top. It was a large volume vessel (fig. 22).

Fig. 22

Hu (壺): These bronze pieces of the Shang and Zhou dynasties had long necks and large bellies, and most of the Western Zhou Dynasty pieces (1046–771 BC) were used to hold wine (fig. 23).

Fig. 23

Lei (罍): There were two kinds of wine containers and ritual vessels in the pre-Qin period, both round and square. The round *lei* had a closing mouth, wide neck, large belly, and either ring foot or a flat bottom. There were either two or four handles on the neck, in the shape of either a ring or an animal head. It had a small protruding portion on the belly. The square *lei* was deep, with a small mouth, sloping shoulders, ring foot (some flat bottom), lids, and small protrusions. The body of the *lei* usually contained many patterns (fig. 24).

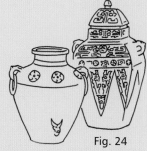

Fig. 24

Gu (觚): Used for drinking, but also as a ritual device, the *gu* had a horn-shaped mouth, slender belly, and high ring foot (fig. 25).

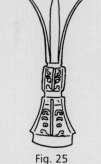

Fig. 25

Zhu Zhanji (reigning from 1425–1435), saw bronzeware pieces placed in suburban temples and the inner Ming courts as having rough shapes, and not of the ancient shape and structure. Very dissatisfied, he sent out an imperial edict for the Ministry of Works to model the bronzeware after the Shang and Zhou dynasties recorded in *Research of Artifacts (Kaogong Tu)*, *Study of the Ancient in the Xuanhe Period*, and other records. In this way, more than 3,300 pieces were made in the first batch. The texture and style were simple, but elegant. Later, Xuanzong ordered another batch. The total number of bronze foundry items reached more than 10,000 pieces, spread all across the country. As a result, the use of bronzeware was expanding, which in turn expanded appreciation of this ancient art form (see fig. 15 on pages 20 and 21). The imitation pieces made by the Ming court were mostly based on Song Dynasty texts, which were not so rigorous. As a result, Ming Dynasty imitations were not as well shaped. Some imitations, though similar in appearance, introduce innovations, many of which result in serious distortions of the pattern, making them quite different from Shang and Zhou dynasties pieces. Even so, generally speaking, the bronzeware of the Ming Dynasty has a charm all its own, and is thus worthy of recognition. In any case, as a vessel for vase flower arrangements, even a piece of ancient bronzeware with distorted shape or pattern is both charming and durable. Its elegant form, calming aura, and ability to store water all make it fit for flower arrangement (see fig. 26 on page 32).

Fig. 26
Antiques and Flowers
Huang Shiling
(1849–1908)
Set color book
Height 28.5 cm ×
Width 41 cm × 4

Huang Shiling was the founder of the Yishan School of carving and an exceptional painter of flowers and antique. The flowers featured in these four paintings are, from top left, the poppy, nandina, tulip, and chrysanthemum. It can be seen from this that the tulip, which originated in Europe, had been introduced into China by this time. This late Qing antique and flower painting appears dull and stiff, lacking the smart, fresh quality of paintings by the Ming Dynasty literati.

The Zhang family owned many antiques. Unearthed bronze vases, bronze bowls, *shuixiu* (fig. 27) and many *chuanshigu* objects could be used for flower arrangement. Zhang Qiande had much experience in this field, and he believed that bronzeware that had been buried was impregnated with a rustic force that made it particularly suited to growing flowers, and they were bright and shiny, as if they too had grown on branches. This sort of elegance was worthy of a nobleman and his family. These families also had a shared sense of the values of the antiques, and so could take them out for viewing with flowers in their spare time. They were both a treasured possession and a vessel to be utilized.

Fig. 27 *Rise in Rank Scroll* (detail)
Chen Hongshou
Ink and color on silk
Height 24.2 cm × Width 235 cm
Palace Museum, Beijing

The *Rise in Rank Scroll* includes nineteen figures, seventeen of whom face the left side, either making a bow with hands folded in front or paying respect to congratulate the man in red at the left end of the picture for his official promotion. This figure on the left holds a vase flower arrangement in hand, which contains pine branches. The bronze vase is visibly mottled with rust.

Fig. 28 *Chrysanthemum*
Huang Shanshou (Qing Dynasty)
The two long stalks of yellow and red chrysanthemum in this painting are held in a vase, with more flowers situated on a plate in front of it and fingered citron placed in the distance. This sort of vase flower was commonly seen in the aristocratic families in the Qing Dynasty.

4. Porcelain Ware and Its Types

The main material used in vessels for flower arrangement, porcelain was divided into two main types, ordinary porcelain and "kiln utensils" from famous kilns (fig. 28). The evaluation of grades of porcelain during the Ming Dynasty was probably based on the Song standards. Of these, the five famous kilns in the Song Dynasty (the Ru, Guan, Ge, Jun, and Ding kilns) were real objects that were well-tested and readily available. Ru Kiln porcelain was considered most valuable. For porcelain of the Ming Dynasty, even pieces from the official kiln of Xuande and Chenghua (1465–1487) were only ranked at the lowest rungs.

Famous Historical Kilns

Chai Kiln. In the later part of the Five Dynasties (907–960), during the Zhou Dynasty (951–960), Emperor Chairong (921–959) established kilns for making finely crafted porcelain, the glaze of which was ranked top in the field, setting a high standard for ancient celadon glaze. The porcelain ware produced at the Chai Kiln and secret color porcelain (a kind of porcelain with celadon glaze) were seen as a "divine product" that could only exist in legends, and thus was rarely seen in the world.

Ru Kiln. This famous Song Dynasty kiln was established during the late Northern Song Dynasty. The kiln was located in the territory of Ruzhou (currently in Ruzhou City and Baofeng County, Henan Province). Famed for firing celadon, its products included wares of azure, pea green, and a pale blue. As an imperial treasure of the royal family of Northern Song Dynasty, the Ru Kiln had a burning process that was unrivalled. After the Jin (1115–1234) overthrow of the Northern Song Dynasty, the kiln was wiped out, lasting only two decades in total. For this reason, not only was the craftsmanship from this kiln the most exquisite of the five, but the wares produced there are also rarest.

Fig. 29 Large Vase from the Guan Kiln

Song Dynasty

This vase has a round mouth, straight neck, wide belly, and ring foot. Its inside and outside are under celadon glaze, and its outside is glazed with ice crack, creating an elegant, dignified style. What is most outstanding about porcelain from the Guan Kiln is its jade-like glaze.

Guan Kiln. Among Song Dynasty porcelain ware, the Guan Kiln is a special name, referring to the celadon made by the court at the kiln located in the capital of the Northern Song Dynasty in Bianjing (now Kaifeng, Henan Province) and of the Southern Song Dynasty (1127–1279) in Lin'an (now Hangzhou, Zhejiang Province). The products in these kilns can be divided into "old Guan" and "new Guan," the former coming from the Northern Song Dynasty Guan Kiln, and the latter from the Southern Song Dynasty Guan Kiln (fig. 29).

Ge Kiln. Of the famed Song Dynasty kilns, very little porcelain is left from this kiln, and its location is unknown, despite its significance in the history of Chinese ceramics (fig. 30).

Ding Kiln. The name for this renowned Song Dynasty kiln arises from its location in the Dingzhou (now Quyang County, Baoding City, Hebei Province) area. The Ding Kiln was originally a folk kiln, forged in the Tang Dynasty. It began burning porcelain for the court in the mid and late Northern Song Dynasty, flourishing in the Northern Song and Jin dynasties, and ending in the Yuan Dynasty. It was renowned for producing white porcelain, and for its black glaze, brown glaze, and glazed porcelain (fig. 31).

Jun Kiln. The official Jun Kiln of the Northern Song Dynasty was symmetrical and elegant, the embodiment of the highest level of craftsmanship in the Northern Song Dynasty (see fig. 39 on page 37).

Longquan Kiln. The main production area for this kiln was named after Longquan City, Zhejiang Province. The Longquan Kiln was founded in the Three Kingdoms Period and closed in the Qing Dynasty. It produced porcelain for 1,600 years, the longest production history for any Chinese porcelain kiln. The Longquan Kiln was famous for firing celadon, with a green glaze. During the Northern Song Dynasty, most of its porcelain

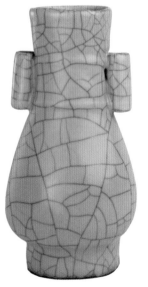

Fig. 30 Ge Kiln Two-Handled Flat Vase

Song Dynasty

Of the five famous kilns, the Ru, Guan, and Ge Kilns had ice crack. The Ru and Guan also had small ice-cracked patterns, while the Ge Kiln had two sizes of patterns. The larger was an iron-black color, and the smaller was beige, called the "Golden Thread."

Fig. 31 Ding Kiln White Glazed Plum Vase with Carved Lotus Pattern

Song Dynasty

This vase has a small mouth, a short neck, and broad shoulders, narrowing from the shoulders down and set on a ring foot. This is commonly known as a "plum vase." It is tall and straight, according to the standard style of the Ding Kiln plum vase in the Song Dynasty.

was glazed pale cyan, while in the Southern Song it was mostly a dark cyan (see fig. 41 on page 37).

Zhangsheng Kiln. At the Song Dynasty Longquan, two brothers from the Zhang household fired porcelain. The oldest brother's kiln was called the Ge Kiln, and the second brother's the Zhang Longquan Kiln, or the Zhang Kiln for short.

Wuni Kiln. The site of this famed Song Dynasty kiln was in Shuiji Town, Jianyang County, Fujian Province. It was famous for its black glazed porcelain.

Xuande Kiln. This kiln in Jingdezhen, renowned during the Ming Dynasty Xuande period, was the highest ranked official kiln during the Ming Dynasty. It was best known for its blue-and-white porcelain (fig. 32).

Chenghua Kiln. Under the Ming Dynasty Emperor Xianzong (reigning from 1464–1487), in the Chenghua period, this kiln operated in Jingdezhen. It was best known for its blue-and-white porcelain as well as *doucai* (overglaze colored enamel) (fig. 33).

Types of Porcelain

Zhang Qiande believed that the ideal shape of any vessel for containing flowers was that it have a "small mouth and a thicker base," in order to keep it stable. He was meticulous in his selection of vessels for the study, listing all sorts of elegant, refined containers, such as ancient pots, bile bottles, *zun*, *gu*, and vases for a single flower. One step down from them were small yarrow bottles, paper mallet bottles, plain round bottles, goose-neck bottles, and the like, which, though

Fig. 32 Xuande Blue-and-White Porcelain Dragon Globular Vase
Ming Dynasty

Modeled on the Syrian style of vase, this piece utilizes the decorative techniques of blue-and-white porcelain, representing waves on a sea of water. A white dragon image rises from the left blank form, while at the same time, dragon details are etched in blue on the dragon body.

not ideal, could also be used. At the same time, there were numerous types of popular Ming Dynasty porcelain that Zhang rejected outright. They included:

Anhua, referring to the use of finer tools to create a pattern on the body of the vessel, so that once the glaze was formed, a clean pattern emerged.

Eggplant bags, commonly known as a purse, which were worn as slim pieces used for change, but which in this instance refers to a type of eggplant-shaped porcelain.

Gourd-shaped containers, referring to a bottle-shaped object like a gourd, which was a traditional type of porcelain. Zhang believed that such bottles didn't "approach decorating used for appreciation," so were not worthy of a gentleman's gaze (fig. 33).

Fig. 33 Chenghua Blue-and-White Porcelain Gourd-Shaped Vase with Carved Lotus Pattern
Ming Dynasty

This gourd-shaped vase is very chic. Its name is a homophone for "good fortune," and it also represents longevity, fertility, giving it many auspicious associations. This resulted in it being frequently used at festivals. This type of vase was not only a popular item among the common people, but was also a favored item of the Ming and Qing courts. This gourd-shaped vase was decorated all over with lotus flowers of Buddhism.

Types of Porcelain Suitable for Flower Arrangement

Fig. 34

Fig. 36

Ancient pot: indicating the earlier pot-shaped porcelain. This gem was made by the Yue Kiln during the Tang Dynasty, when porcelain manufacturing was at its apex (fig. 34).

Gallbladder-shaped bottle: named for its bile-like shape, this vessel had a straight mouth and a slender neck, making it ideal for flower arrangements. The gallbladder-shaped bottle began in the Tang Dynasty and carried through the Song. It was a typical type of ceramic flower vase. The glaze of this Song Dynasty Ge Kiln gallbladder-shaped bottle was subtle and crystal clear, with crisscrossing patterns, changing naturally and with rich tones (fig. 35).

Fig. 35

Zun: A large or medium sized wine container formed during the Shang and Zhou dynasties, mostly made of bronze, but later adapted to porcelain designs. The moon-white glazed *zun* vessel with vertical ridges of the Song Dynasty Jun Kiln was the typical porcelain used at court during the Song Dynasty (fig. 36). The kiln was used mainly to fire flower pots at the time. The shape of the ancient bronze *zun* had a flared mouth, flat drum-shaped belly, and an outer ring foot. All sides of the neck, abdomen, and base had bars along the squared edges, commonly known as "vertical ridges."

Gu: a container mostly for drinking,

Fig. 37

usually made of bronze, then later adapted to porcelain styling. The sculptural characteristics of these vases include a ring foot, open mouth, and long body, with trumpet-shaped mouth and base. This is an example of Ming Dynasty blue-and-white porcelain (fig. 37).

Fig. 38

Small yarrow bottle: a type of bottle modeled after ancient jade *cong*. The square on the outside represents the earth, and the circle inside represents the heavens, indicating that the vessel was used in ancient rituals to connect heaven and earth, making it an important tool. In the Southern Song Dynasty, imitation of jade *cong* porcelain pieces were used in the study for flower arrangements. Influenced by the Taoist culture of the Ming Dynasty, these bottles were often decorated with the *bagua* pattern, and were sometimes used as containers for yarrow and divination sticks. These enamel vessels were known as "*shicao* bottles" or "*bagua* bottles." Among them, the *cong*-style bottles made at the Longquan Kiln was the most exquisite (fig. 38).

Fig. 39

Paper-mallet bottle: a straight-necked vase named for a paper-making tool (fig. 39).

Plain round bottle: referring to a round-bodied vase. This was the Song Dynasty Ge Kiln's celadon vase with bowstring patterns (fig. 40).

Gooseneck wall bottle: the rear side of this vase was almost perfectly flat, allowing it to be hung on a wall or carriage. This type of object was an innovation of the Ming Dynasty Wanli period. The bottle's name refers to its long, curved neck (fig. 41).

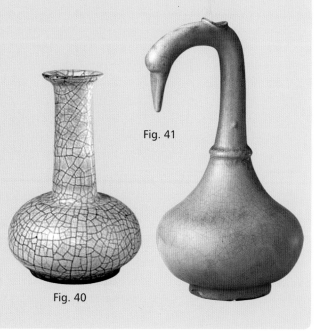

Fig. 41

Fig. 40

Small opening, referring to a narrow-mouthed bottle with a long, thin neck, which was a popular form of Ming Dynasty porcelain.

Flat-belly bottle, a vessel with a slender neck and flat, round abdomen, shaped like a water chestnut, popular in the Ming and Qing dynasties, such as the ribbon moon bottle during the Yongxuan period of the Ming Dynasty. This is the period in which Emperor Chengzu, Zhu Di (1360–1424), and subsequently Renzong (1378–1425) and Xuanzong ruled.

Thin-bottomed medicine jar, referring to vessels used for containing medicine. In the Ming Dynasty, these pots were generally porcelain, and had thin bottoms, which meant that the bottom was thinner, much as the plum vase is known for its slim bottom.

5. Winter Decorations for Appreciation: Plum Blossom

Zhang Qinade specifically pointed out that large vases could be used to hold plum blossom. This was an elegant arrangement with a long, and appealing cultural tradition.

The composition for arrangements using plum blossom was different for that of other flowers. The peony held a sort of national charm and heavenly fragrance, with a large flower appreciated for its color and flamboyance, so a peony placed in a vase represented prosperity. The magnolia was elegant and white, so a magnolia in a vase highlighted its slim, and graceful bearing. Peach and apricot flowers were tender and colorful, so displaying these flowers in a vase created a lively feel. Plum blossoms had their

The Evolution of Vase Shapes

In Zhang Qiande's use of the words "ancient pot," his meticulous nature is seen.

The ancient pots dating before the Ming Dynasty were quite different from those popular in Zhang's time. The Tang Dynasty white glazed pots from the Xing Kiln, the celadon pots of the Yue Kiln, and the unearthed porcelain pots dating from the Han Dynasty (206 BC–AD 220) were quite suitable for flower arrangement. Taking the Tang Dynasty celadon pot of the Yue Kiln as an example, it had a wide mouth, a short neck, slick body, and bulging belly. Filled with white chrysanthemums or gardenias, it created a very harmonious arrangement (see fig. 34 on page 36).

The porcelain pots of the Ming Dynasty were similar to modern teapots, and they are known more for tea-brewing than for flower arrangements. Pieces such as the early-Ming

Fig. 42 Red Banana Pattern Ewer with Underglaze Red Design
Ming Dynasty

Dynasty underglaze-red porcelain pot with plantain design, with a fine handle and a slender mouth, represented the typical shape of a Ming Dynasty porcelain pot (fig. 42).

It is also evident that, though these pots were used in the Tang Dynasty for storing wine and making tea, it was also quite appropriate to use them for flower arrangements. But during the Ming Dynasty, it was used only for making tea.

Fig. 43 *Palace Gossip*
Chen Hongshou
Height 93.4 cm × Width 46.8 cm
Ink and color on paper
Shenyang Palace Museum

This painting, based on the story of the late Eastern Han Dynasty figure Ling Xuan, was painted after the end of the Ming Dynasty. Ling Xuan served as an officer of the Han Dynasty, and his concubine, Fan Tongde, was a palace maid who, familiar with the affairs of Emperor Chengdi, often related stories of the palace to Ling Xuan, who subsequently handed them down as *Rumors of Zhao Feiyan.* This painting means to depict the so-called "white haired palace maid sitting and speaking of Xuanzong." In it, the woman holds scrolls, and an ice-crack porcelain vase occupies the stand. It is full of plum blossoms. Just opposite the woman is a scholar, looking dignified. He seems to be recalling old stories and bygone places, which is precisely what the Ming Dynasty literati are thinking after the end of the Ming Dynasty.

own style, so the composition and concept of an arrangement of plum blossoms had to make good use of crossing old, thin branches (fig. 43).

There were many things to consider when arranging plum blossoms in a vase. It was best to use a vessel of dark or plain colors, but without few patterns. Antique bronze and porcelain vases would best show the elegance of plum blossom. The blossoms were not placed in extravagant vases, to avoid distracting viewers. Only one branch of plum blossom was to be used in an arrangement, displaying its elegant, solitary height. If many branches were inserted, the blossoms would become too numerous and varied, looking like peach or apricot flowers, which is not the style of plum blossoms.

In addition to laying out this aesthetic, Zhang Qiande also mentions the maintenance of floral materials. Sulfur was used mainly as a medicinal material in ancient times. Ming Dynasty experts in the horticultural arts discovered that when it was cold, sulfur powder could be put in vases to prevent freezing. In fact, putting sulfur in a flower arrangement water effectively prevents rot of the peduncle, reduces the decay rate of the stalk, and extends the plant's period of flowering.

CHAPTER 2
APPRECIATING FLOWERS

THE ORIGINAL TEXT

The Book of Flowers (*Hua Jing*) uses nine ranks to determine the level of flowers. This approach was started by my ancestor in the house of Zhang. (In ancient times, people were called by different names before and after death. The name by which he was called after death required great thought, as it must show "honor, affection, and wisdom." This name applied by Zhang Qiande indicates that he was an ancestor of the Zhang family and, as a matter of respect, Zhang Qiande could not call him by his full name.) He was a master with the pen, and truly captured floral scenes on paper. Today, as I offer instructions on vase flower arrangements, according to the ways of my predecessors, I should rank the flowers in order to record these dozens of decorations for appreciation in a way that is clear, and should use the "nine grades and nine tiers" to rank them.

Among the flowers of Grade One, Tier Nine are the orchid, peony, plum blossom, wintersweet, all types of chrysanthemums, narcissus, camellia from Yunnan, winter daphne, and sweet flag or calamus.

Among those of Grade Two, Tier Eight are cymbidium, rosa rubus, kaido crabapple, jasmine, yellow and white camellia, osmanthus, *bailing*, pine twig, banana shrub, and camellia.

Among those of Grade Three, Tier Seven are herbaceous peony, amygdalus persica, lotus, lilac, camellia from Sichuan, and bamboo.

Among those of Grade Four, Tier Six are symplocos, magnolia coco, pearl orchid, rose (rosa multiflora), begonia, common mallow, apricot flower, magnolia liliflora, various types of pomegranates, Chinese hibiscus, and pear blossoms.

Among those of Grade Five, Tier Five are rugosa rose (rosa rugosa), campaka, crape myrtle, long yellow daylily, tawny daylily, and fragrant nutmeg.

Among those of Grade Six, Tier Four are magnolia, winter jasmine, hibiscus, royal jasmine, willow twigs and sasanqua camellia.

Among those of Grade Seven, Tier Three are Chinese pea shrub, rhododendron molle, wolfberry, garden balsam, Chinese plum, citrus aurantium flower, and azaleas.

Among those of Grade Eight, Tier Two are hollyhock, hosta plantaginea, cockscomb, China pink, malus pumila flower, and sunset muskmallow.

Among those of Grade Nine, Tier One are lychnis coronate (rose campion), lychnis fulgens (brilliant campion), lesser galangal, dianthus, morning glory, chaenomeles cathayensis, and lophatherum.

On pages 41–43

Figs. 44–47 *One Hundred Flowers* (detail)
Yun Shouping (1633–1690)
Ink and color on silk
Height 41.9 cm × Width 649 cm
The Metropolitan Museum of Art, New York

This section of the *One Hundred Flowers* handscroll is a brush color set of purple peony, plum blossom, camellia, magnolia, and other flowers representing the four seasons.

THE MODERN READER

In Chinese culture, almost every traditional flower is stamped with a unique, unchanging culturally symbolic value. The appreciation of flowers is not only the appreciation of the color of the flowers before one's eyes, but also of a beautiful, delicate cultural mood.

Zhang Qiande praised Zhang Yi's *Book of Flowers* and used it to categorize seventy-one species of flowers. Arranged according to quality, from top down, the system was modeled after official rankings, and was thus divided according to "nine grades and nine tiers." ("Nine tiers" refers to the nine levels of the Zhou Dynasty [1046–256 BC] officials, with the highest being called "Tier Nine" and the lowest as "Tier One." After the Wei and Jin dynasties, the official ranking was from one grade to nine, with one being the highest.) This was intended to open up the "flower rank" and "flower spectrum" for future generations. Zhang Qiande arranged the flowers according to this system, recording the ranks by which dozens of types of flowers could be used in decorations for appreciation (figs. 44–47).

The Book of Flowers and Zhang Yi

There is some disagreement in the records regarding Zhang Yi, author of the *Book of Flowers*. According to the text itself, Zhang Yi was born to an official family in Chang'an, and was shielded from the chaos of war at the end of the Tang Dynasty only by fleeing to Jiangnan. During the Southern Tang Dynasty period (937–975), Zhang Yi attained the high official position of Xichang, and it was a rather glorious time for him. He was a man of great political achievement, and eloquent in his works of literary criticism. He had many official achievements, but with poorly cultivated character, he was extreme, impetuous and arrogant, bullying his subordinates. He was ultimately poisoned and died a terrible death. In his own text, Zhang Qiande called Zhang Yi his ancestor. If true, it indicates that the Ming Dynasty Zhang family had a very long history in the Kunshan area.

The Book of Flowers list the following grades of flowers:

Grade One, Tier Nine: orchid, peony, wintersweet, rosa rubus, and winter daphne.

Grade Two, Tier Eight: Chinese snowball, cymbidium, cinnamomum pauciflorum, jasmine, and banana shrub.

Grade Three, Tier Seven: herbaceous

peony, lotus, campaka, lilac, flowering peach, hall crabapple, and amygdalus persica.

Grade Four, Tier Six: chrysanthemum, apricot, magnolia liliflora, fragrant nutmeg, clerodendrum trichotomum, tawny daylily, cerasus pseudocerasus, malus pumila flower, and plum blossoms.

Grade Five, Tier Five: poplar blossom, Moon Red (*Yuehong*), pear blossom, Chinese plum, peach blossom, and pomegranate.

Grade Six, Tier Four: Gathering Eight Immortals (*Jubaxian*), Gold Sand (*Jinsha*), *Baoxiang* rose, crape myrtle, Chinese trumpet vine, and crabapple.

Grade Seven, Tier Three: Spreading Flower (*Sanhua*), Pure Bead (*Zhenzhu*), viburnum plicatum, oriental bush cherry, rose, symplocos, papaya, camellia, winter Jasmine, rugosa rose, Chinese lantern, Yulania liliiflora, garden balsam, magnolia coco, rhododendron molle, inula flower, weigela, and peperomia blanda.

Grade Eight, Tier Two: azalea, Great Purity (*Daqing*), Dew (*Dilu*), erythrina variegata, magnolia, cockscomb, and *Jinbeidui* rose.

Grade Nine, Tier One: hibiscus, morning glory, hibiscus syriacus, sunflower, hollyhock, calystegia sepium, China pink, and Chinese globe flower.

1. Grade One

In Zhang Qiande's critique and rankings of flowers, those ranked as Grade One, Tier Nine included the orchid, peony, plum blossom, wintersweet, all types of chrysanthemum, narcissus, camellia from Yunnan, winter daphne, and calamus. The orchid, peony, and plum blossom topped the list. These three flowers were renowned throughout the world, and thus were the indisputable leaders on the list. There are several other types of seasonal flowers on the "Grade One" list as well, including the winter blooming wintersweet, the autumn chrysanthemum, the summer calamus, and the spring narcissus.

Orchid. The use of orchids in traditional flower arrangements was rare. Where orchids were cultivated in a cluster, only a few flowers bloomed, as it is only with reluctance that one would cut them to be placed in a vase when they were open. As a result, orchids were mostly used in bonsai settings, rather than in vase flower arrangements (fig. 48).

Peony. Naturally aromatic, the peony is startlingly beautiful, like a beautifully adorned woman, so that these flowers were often used in floral arrangements for the palace, such as that depicted by the Emperor Xuanzong, Zhu Zhanji in *The Rich Vase* (see fig. 148 on page 114). In the aristocratic tradition, the peony was often inserted into a bronze pot, from

which we can also see the Ming style of vase flower arrangements. In the Tang Dynasty, the peony was used in conjunction with the ladies of the court. In Ming Dynasty figure paintings of ladies, the peony was often used in the company of aristocratic ladies.

Plum blossom. The plum is a full tree with many branches. Finely arranged, it can have a heroic appearance. The *Portrait of the Late Xinguogong* (*Translator's note*: Xinguogong is an official title), by Yuan Dynasty artist Qian Xuan (c. 1239–c. 1300), makes use of the plum blossom to depict the loyalty of Wen Tianxiang (1236–1283), the Southern Song Dynasty literary scholar and minister against the Yuan reign (fig. 49).

Wintersweet. This flower was an indispensable embellishment in decorations of the study for winter days. The most elegant

Fig. 48 *Ink Orchid*
Zhao Mengjian (1199–before 1267)
Ink on paper
Height 34.5 cm × Width 90.2 cm
Palace Museum, Beijing

In this painting, long leaves radiate and scatter, crossing one another as they stretch across the page, revealing the artist's solitary, refined mental realm. Zhao Mengjian was an exceptional poet, and his family owned an excellent collection. His excellent depictions of plum blossom, orchids, bamboo, rocks, and the generous use of ink in his paintings created an elegant style that won the praise of the literati.

use of the wintersweet was to place a bouquet of it in a porcelain vase on the desk.

Chrysanthemum. This plant family includes both the autumn and winter chrysanthemum. Horticultural cultivation of the chrysanthemum was a well-developed art by the Ming Dynasty. More than 270 varieties of chrysanthemum had been collected and introduced by the scholar and agronomist Wang Xiangjin in *Book of Horticulture (Erru Ting Qunfang Pu)*, where he offered an introduction to plant cultivation. It is evident that there was an abundant supply of flowers at the time. In the late Ming Dynasty, the literati generally liked to use chrysanthemum in flower arrangements as

Fig. 49 *Portrait of the Late Xinguogong*

Qian Xuan
Ink and color on silk
Height 140 cm × Width 60 cm

Qian Xuan, a famous painter in the late Song, early Yuan period, was known collectively with Zhao Mengfu as "Eight Scholars of Wuxing." He was a poet and a master calligrapher and painter. He advocated "morale" in his paintings, and wrote poems or postscripts on his works, sprouting a form of literati paintings that has integrates poetry, calligraphy and painting as one of its main characteristics.

a symbol of seclusion and nobility. With regard to paintings by Eastern Jin Dynasty poet Tao Yuanming (365 or 372 or 376–427), one cannot overstate the importance of the chrysanthemum, presenting the image of a recluse enjoying the pastoral landscape and staying detached from the hustle and bustle of the urban life.

Narcissus. Since the Yuan and Song dynasties, most vases depicted in paintings for the Spring Festival have included the narcissus. Because its flowering period comes right at the end of the lunar year, raising a pot of narcissus allows one to welcome the New Year. In ancient paintings of the decorations for appreciation at the end of lunar year, this flower is absolutely indispensable.

Camellia from Yunnan. This category refers specifically to varieties of camellia from Yunnan. During the Jiajing period of the Ming Dynasty, it is likely that the camellia native to Jiangnan and other places was transplanted from Sichuan and Yunnan. They were called *shucha* and *diancha*, respectively. The geographer Xu Xiake (1587–1641) wrote in his travelogue *Flowers of Yunnan* (*Dianzhong Huamu Ji*), "The camellia is larger than a bowl, and clustered like a ball, with the best type featuring septum, curled edges, and soft twigs." It is evident that the Yunnan camellia was greatly cherished in Jiangnan gardens during the Ming Dynasty.

Winter daphne. Flowers in the Daphne family are very fragrant and have very large leaves. In their use for vase flower arrangements, they could only be used as complementary adornment for ritual offerings. To avoid a confusion of aromas, they are not to be used with other fragrant flowers.

Calamus. This plant is a perennial herb, and falls under the general category of Araceae Acorus. Such plants are suitable for both vase flower arrangements and bonsai. It could be arranged in two ways.

Fig. 50　*Vase Flower for Dragon Boat Festival*
Giuseppe Castiglione
Ink and color on silk
Height 140 cm × Width 84 cm
Palace Museum, Beijing

In this piece, the main material of the vase flower arrangement is pomegranate and hollyhock, with calamus leaves and mugwort lining the background.

The first was to take the sword-shaped leaves of the calamus and arrange them as either the primary or complementary feature; the second was to use acorus tatarinowii as a bonsai, to be accompanied with flower arrangement. In the folk custom of Jiangnan areas, every household prepared arrangements of mugwort and calamus during the Dragon Boat Festival (fig. 50).

2. Grade Two

The flowers Zhang Qiande categorized as Grade Two Tier Eight include flowers commonly used in Ming Dynasty Jiangnan gardens, particularly the kaido crabapple, osmanthus, and camellia. Because these three types of plants and flowers were used in gardens, it was also convenient to use them in vase flower arrangements. As for *bailing*, pine twig, and banana shrub, these three types of flowers were relatively rare.

Cymbidium. This refers to the herbaceous of cymbidium and orchidaceae, a family of plants that are the oldest and most popular species of orchid cultivated in China. The group includes the traditional cymbidium orchid called "cymbidium," the cymbidium ensifolium blossoming in autumn called "autumn cymbidium," and the cymbidium hookerianum originating in the southwest called the "large flowering cymbidium."

Orchids and cymbidium belong to the same genera, both being herbaceous plants. The differences between the two are that the orchid has one flower per stem and its aroma is rich. The cymbidium has multiple flowers on each stem and is less fragrant. Ancient scholars valued the orchid more highly than the cymbidium. In ancient times, the names of these two flowers were often used interchangeably, even though the orchid was more highly valued.

Rosa rubus. This flower is in fact a white rose, a small shrub with white flowers, which are small and grow densely on the bush. They have a rich fragrance, and can be used in a vase floral arrangement placed on the desk, where they look very elegant. Song Dynasty scholars preferred this flower and wrote many songs and verses about it. For instance,

Fig. 51 **Crabapple**
Lu Zhi (1496–1576)
Ink and color on silk
Height 18.3 cm × Width 53 cm (fan)
Palace Museum, Taibei

Lu Zhi, a Wuxian (now Suzhou, Jiangsu Province) native, was skilled in poem and ancient texts. His landscapes painting were influenced by the Wumen School, infused with his own style and novel ideas. Many researchers believe this piece features two sprigs of peach blossoms, but because the twigs have long pedicels and oval leaves, it is more likely that the flowers featured are crabapples in spring.

the Southern Song Dynasty scholar Xin Qiji (1140–1207) wrote, "A trace of spring remains even when all the white roses are plucked." Ancient scholars believed this was the last flower to open in the spring. When it opened, it meant spring was drawing to an end.

Kaido crabapple. This small tree of the genus Rosaceae is named after Xifu (now Baoji City, Shaanxi Province), the place where it grows. It is one of China's traditional flowers. Ancient scholars ranked the varieties of its flowers from high to low, even within the same species (fig. 51). For crabapple, kaido crabapple, hall crabapple, flowering quince, and chaenomeles cathayensis were collectively known as "the four grades of crabapple." The kaido crabapple was the most highly valued of the four.

***Baozhu* (Jewelry) jasmine**. A type of jasmine, it is a bi-petal cultivated flower growing on a small shrub of up to one meter in height. It blooms in early summer, with a white corolla, and is an aromatic flower.

Yellow and white camellia. Most camellia are red, while the yellow and white varieties are quite rare, making them more highly prized. Some of the yellow varieties are known as "golden tea flowers" or "the queen of tea." The yellow-flower camellia is depicted in the painting *Camellia and Bird* (fig. 52).

Similar to the camellia is the *diancha*, which Zhang Qiande listed among the Grade One, Tier Nine category, while listing the yellow- and white-flower camellia as Grade Two, Tier Eight. *Diancha* is the common name for the camellia from Yunnan, which also includes the white- and the yellow-flowered camellias. This was an oversight on Zhang's part.

Osmanthus. The osmanthus is often referred to in poetry as *muxi* (meaning tree rhinoceros), while *yangui* (meaning rock osmanthus) was the term preferred by Northern Song Dynasty philosopher and educator Zhu Xi (1130–1200). The osmanthus grows among mountains and rocks. There are some with leaves that are jagged, crooked, and coarse, like those of the loquats', while there have leaves that are smooth and clean, with no sawtooths, like those found in the gardenia. The white flowers are called silver, the yellow, gold, and the red, orange osmanthus. The sweet-scented osmanthus was ideal for garden courts.

Bailing. It is difficult to determine with any certainty which flower is referred to by this term. According to agricultural information recorded in *Book of Various Flowers* (*Guangqun Fangpu*), this flower originated in Yuzhang (now Nanchang, Jiangxi Province). Unable to tolerate cold weather, it must be kept warm and indoors all winter. The term might refer to a small shrub that blooms in summer and autumn, flowering with thousands of petals and leaves. Its leaves appear together with the flowers, and there is one flower per branch, cradled by numerous leaves. It blooms in July and

Fig. 52 *Camellia and Bird*
Zhou Shuxi (Ming Dynasty)
Ink and color on silk
Height 43 cm × Width 26.9 cm
Nanjing Museum

This painting depicts a variety of camellia, the gorgeous golden yellow flower. The bloom is depicted upside down, due to the bent stalk. Zhou Shuxi was a female painter of the Ming Dynasty, from Jiangyin in Jiangsu Province. She excelled at bird and flower and insect paintings, using the brush like a silkworm making silk. Her works reflect a brightly colored, vivid charm.

August. Its flowers are the color of white jade, and as delicate. In ancient times, there was no uniform standard for the classification and naming of flowers and trees. Some were named differently by different people, and the same name was often used to indicate different flowers. This is a regrettable fact.

Pine twigs. Pine twigs were often used in flower arrangements, particularly in the Ming and Qing dynasties. The pine twig retains its splendor in all seasons, so can be used to supplement a variety of vase flower arrangements. It can also be displayed on its own (fig. 53).

Banana shrub. It belongs to the family of Magnoliaceae. It is an evergreen shrub, about two to three meters tall. Its flower is fragrant and luxuriant. It is most commonly used for greenery in a courtyard. During the Ming Dynasty, it was also used in flower arrangements.

Camellia. The camellia was often used in scenes within a Ming Dynasty Jiangnan garden. During the Ming Dynasty, gardening culture flourished, and many new types of camellia were recorded.

3. Grade Three

Herbaceous peony. The peony and herbaceous peony are similar, but one is a woody plant and the other herbaceous plant. Both are large, rich, elegant, luxurious plants, but they are of different grades. The peony is ranked Grade One, Tier Nine, while the herbaceous peony is ranked Grade Three, Tier Seven, a full two grades lower. The herbaceous peony grows in the Jiangnan region and especially flourishes around Yangzhou (Jiangsu Province). It is often said that "the herbaceous peony in Yangzhou is the best of all."

Amygdalus persica. Peach trees are divided into two categories: flowering and fruiting. In the flowering variety, flowers are primary. The flowering peach are collectively called amygdalus persica. In the Tang and Song dynasties, amygdalus persica were planted beside the palace walls, so that the large, double-flanked, layered flowers could spread their fragrance throughout the palace.

Lotus. The lotus was commonly used in floral arrangements by the Ming Dynasty literati to stand for a noble person. Chen Hongshou, also known as "Lao Lian (meaning old lotus)," preferred to place lotus flowers in a copper bottle. He believed the lotus was commensurate with the spirit of the

Fig. 53 *Luohan Scratching Back Mending Clothing*
Song Xu (Ming Dynasty)
Ink and color on silk
Height 219.7 cm × Width 86.4 cm
Asian Art Museum, San Francisco

In the early morning as the sun rises, beneath a palm tree sits a monk holding a needle and thread, with which he sews a garment. A servant in blue clothing stands respectfully beside him, while another monk on the other side of him, naked from the waist up, and appears to be extremely comfortable. It is worth noting that a blue glazed vase stands behind the monk and the servant, holding pine branches from the mountain slopes, a perfect match to the monk.

Fig. 54 *Noble Scholars Holding Lotus*

Chen Hongshou
Ink and color on silk
Height 134.5 cm × Width 60 cm

This painting was made in celebration of the birthday of Lu Shanglan, from Pinghu, Jiaxing, Zhejiang Province. Chen Hongshou painted a noble scholar holding a lotus, pointing to a person who has good character despite his corrupt surroundings. Lu Shanglan was a renowned member of the Fu She, a poetry society, of the Ming Dynasty literati. Chen Hongshou used the lotus as a metaphor for his noble personality, likening him to a clear stream flowing through a dirty world.

nobility, prompting the creation of figure paintings such as *Noble Scholars Holding Lotus* (fig. 54), in which lotus flowers were depicted in copper bottles. The flowers depicted were in full bloom, with green leaves and an ancient, weathered feel.

Lilac. This flower was loved by the Tang Dynasty literati. In Tang poetry, the lilac was used to represent deep attachment and two hearts beating as one. There is mutual understanding, and naturally there is also bitterness, so the lilac is often accompanied by "heart knots," implying a certain sort of emotional complexity.

***Shucha* or Camellia from Sichuan**. This term refers to the camellia transplanted from Sichuan to Jiangnan. This is the third time the camellia appears in Zhang Qiande's rankings, demonstrating the position this flower held in gardens and among ornamental plants.

Bamboo. Bamboo stalks make good material for flower arrangements. It was often used in the free-style flower arrangements of the Ming Dynasty literati (fig. 55).

Fig. 55 *Boy Child Worshipping Buddha*
Chen Hongshou
Ink and color on silk
Height 150 cm × Width 67.3 cm
Palace Museum, Beijing

In this painting, a group of children at play in a courtyard mimics prayers. The boy offering flowers holds a couple of chrysanthemums in a white glazed porcelain vase embellished with a few bamboo branches. Their blaze suggests a childlike innocence.

4. Grade Four

Apricot, magnolia, and pear blossoms are all spring flowers, while common mallow, pomegranate flower, and Chinese hibiscus are summer flowers. They can be used in decorations for ritual, and can often be used together. For placement in the study, a pair of stalks can be inserted into a vase. Colorful pomegranate flowers in a vase are particularly suited to brightening up the atmosphere in a room.

Symplocos. The symplocos is a shrub or small tree. There are around 300 species of symplocos, about 80 of which are native to China. This particular variety probably refers to the symplocos paniculata (fig. 56). It is an unusually small tree, but it is exceptionally beautiful when it flowers. It is described in *Compendium of Materia Medica* (*Bencao Gangmu*) as, "blossoming in March with flowers white as snow, each with six yellow pistils, and very fragrant." This type of tree is usually found in the mountains, where it grows slowly. In ancient man-made gardens, they were mostly found in the wild and transplanted, often alongside spring flowers such as plum blossoms or azalea. According to the records of Huang Tingjian, the Northern

Song Dynasty poet and calligrapher, this sort of flower grows in the mountains, blooming in spring, and is very fragrant. The Northern Song Dynasty politician, writer, and thinker, Wang Anshi (1021–1086) once made plans to transport the flower back to his home. Forgetting the name of the flower, Huang Tingjian dubbed it the *shanfan*. It should be displayed in vases, a practice probably begun in the Song Dynasty. In the verse of Song Dynasty poet Li Qi, we read, "When the plum blossom has faded and the peach bloomed, the symplocos is just right for plucking and placing in a vase." He felt that once the plum blossom had passed, there were no flowers suitable for a vase arrangement. Feeling the peach blossom not elegant enough, he asked for a couple of symplocos flowers to be placed in his vase.

Magnolia coco. The small trees of the Magnolia genus are both petite and exquisite. In the summer, its green and white globular flowers bloom. They open in the morning and close at night, but their fragrance is more prevalent at night. It is a flowering plant renowned for its fragrance (fig. 58). Compared with the magnolia, the magnolia coco is smaller and more elegant, and its flowers easier to pluck, making it more suitable for a vase flower arrangement. Song Dynasty artist Li Song's work *Flower Basket* (fig. 57) depicts three large green and white flowers. These are often taken for magnolias or magnolia grandiflora, but the shape of the bud suggests they are actually magnolia coco. They are shown alongside pomegranate flower, indicating that it is early summer, which is certainly not the time for the magnolia to flower. The magnolia grandiflora, with mellow petals, flowers in early summer, but its tree is tall, reaching up to several feet. It is a large tree, rising out of the ground, probably too big for collecting a few flowers for a flower basket, which would likely make the blooms lose their elegance.

Fig. 56 Symplocos Paniculata

Fig. 58　Magnolia Coco

Fig. 57　*Flower Basket*
Li Song (Southern Song Dynasty)
Ink and color on silk
Height 19.1 cm × Width 26.5 cm
Palace Museum, Beijing

Flower Basket is a set of four paintings, one each for spring, summer, autumn, and winter. This piece is the summer painting, depicting flowers commonly used to represent summer, including hollyhock, pomegranate, tawny daylily, and magnolia coco. The magnolia coco is more rounded than the magnolia, with a blue-green outer layer and a white inner layer. Three are used in this painting, one just bloomed and the other two still buds.

Fig. 59　Pearl Orchid

Pearl orchid. This is a small evergreen shrub of the Chloranthus family. Its flower is like a bead, and it is as fragrant as an orchid. A grouping of two or three branches of this flower is quite suitable for placement in a small porcelain vase (fig. 59).

Rose. This type of flower was common in Ming Dynasty gardens. Often used on trellises, it was often known as "a trellis of roses" or "a full trellis of roses." These flowers create a very romantic landscape, full of all the charm of Jiangnan. It is ideal for a landscape garden.

Fig. 60   Begonia

Fig. 62   Magnolia Liliflora

Begonia. This perennial flower of the Begonia family is also known as the "heartbroken flower," and the ancients often used it to refer to pain in love. The begonia is an herbaceous flower with beautifully colored blooms. It is quite impressive when included in a vase flower arrangement (fig. 60).

Common mallow. This perennial flower of the Malva genus blooms in the summer. Its flower is brilliantly colored, and its corolla is purple or white (fig. 61).

Apricot. The apricot flowers in spring. In the capital of the Southern Song Dynasty at Lin'an, it was customary to sell apricot blossoms on spring days, as expressed in the words of the famous poet Lu You (1125–1210), "When spring rains are heard all night in the pavilion, the winding alleys will be full of apricot blossom sellers."

Magnolia liliflora. This deciduous tree of the Magnolia family stands several feet tall, and its wood is aromatic. It is commonly called the purple magnolia. With its purple tones, the magnolia liliflora looks very majestic in a vase. Its buds are shaped like the nibs of wooden pens, making it very attractive and elegant (figs. 62 and 65).

Pomegranate flower. This is used mainly for flower appreciation, comes in many varieties (fig. 63).

Chinese Hibiscus. This evergreen shrub is of the Malvaceae genus (fig. 64).

Fig. 61   Common Mallow

Fig. 63   Pomegranate Flower

Fig. 64   Hibiscus

Fig. 65 *Purple Magnolia Liliflora* (detail)
Chen Chun (Ming Dynasty)
Ink and color on silk
Height 121 cm × Width 58.5 cm

Tang Dynasty poet Wang Wei (c. 701–761) writes in his poem *Xinyiwu*, "At the tip of the twigs, the magnolia blossom; with no one in the cottage in the mountains, the flowers bloom and wither unnoticed." It was from this poem that the magnolia liliflora's reputation grew, and many sorts of magnolia liliflora appeared in Ming Dynasty gardens. Chen Chun painted many magnolia liliflora that, though small, were full of flowers, and their branches always remained small and fine.

Pear blossom. Pear blossoms, like those of the apricot, were often used in Song Dynasty vase flower arrangements, as seen in the words of Southern Song Dynasty poet Fang Yuanji, "The old monk does not understand the wounds of spring, and so uses many pear blossoms as decoration for appreciation." In saying this, he means that older monk often picked pear blossoms to place before the Buddha as decorative pieces. The Song Dynasty poet Wang Zhidao also writes a poem, referring to the practice of picking pear blossoms as a way of prolonging the spring.

Flowers of the Malvaceae Family

The common mallow, hollyhock, and Chinese hibiscus are all similar in shape. These three flowers, which all belong to the Malvaceae family, are often mistaken for one another.

The main difference is the genus each belongs to. The Chinese hibiscus is a woody shrub, while the common mallow and hollyhock are herbaceous plants. Hollyhocks are tall, large, and colorful, while the common mallow is smaller and its leaves slightly different.

There are about 75 genera and 1,000 to 1,500 species of plants in the Malvaceae family, and these are widely distributed in temperate and tropical regions. China is home to 16 genera, 81 species, and 36 varieties. From the perspective of gardening applications, Malvaceae plants have been widely used in Jiangnan gardens since the Ming Dynasty. Hollyhock and common mallow were both popular in gardens. Since both of them flowers during the Dragon Boat Festival, these herbaceous flowers are commonly used as flowers for the appreciation of the festival, often in a vase alongside pomegranate flowers, calamus, and mugwort.

The Gardenia and the Campaka

The term "campaka," coming from Sanskrit, is another name for the gardenia, and Zhang Qiande uses both names in his writing. However, there is still a question regarding whether the gardenia is the same as the campaka introduced into China from the West. The question requires some research into the history of the plants.

After the Eastern Han Dynasty, as Buddhism spread eastward, some plants related to the new religion were introduced. Campaka was among them. This occurred mainly during the Northern and Southern Dynasties (420–589) until the early Tang Dynasty, as there are no records of campaka in early writings. During the Tang Dynasty, the campaka began to appear often in poetry, being a flower that represented spirituality in Buddhism. It was guarded by poisonous snakes, and even woodcutter living in the mountains did not dare to pluck it.

So how did the confusion of this plant arise? The gardenia is very fragrant, as is the campaka, and though the gardenia is commonly seen, the campaka is rarer. This led some people to assume that the term "campaka" in poetry actually referred to the gardenia. Ever since, it was passed on that "campaka" was another name for the gardenia, but in fact, no one really knows for sure what the term pointed to.

This mistaken historical background persisted until the late Tang Dynasty campaign to eliminate Buddhism, known as "the Tang emperor kills the

Fig. 66 *Summer Rugosa Roses*

Chen Chun
Ink and color on paper
Height 122.5 cm × Width 30.5 cm

Suzhou native Chen Chun was a disciple of Wen Zhengming. He was a member of the Wumen School and was especially skilled at freehand flowers.

5. Grade Five

Among the items in Grade Five are rugosa roses, campaka, crape myrtle, long yellow daylily, tawny daylily, and fragrant nutmeg. With the exception of rugosa roses, these plants were much loved by Chinese poets and painters.

Rugosa rose. In ancient times, the flower was not highly regarded by the literati, but was often used as a flavoring for food in the Jiangnan region. During the Song Dynasty,

Buddha," which was a huge blow to Buddhism. The campaka was originally a Buddhist flower often planted in the temple, and

Fig. 67 Champak

Fig. 68 Gardenia

when the temples were destroyed, the flowers were left with no one to care for them. During the Song Dynasty, the literati were only able to associate it with the gardenia, which they called "the friend of Zen." Since then, the gardenia has replaced the campaka as the flower used for sacrifices in Buddhist rituals.

However, according to some scholars, the true campaka may be champak, a member of the Magnolia family, a tall tree scattered across China, India, Nepal, Myanmar, and Vietnam which are all indeed the old strongholds of Buddhism. The champak is the *Michelia champaca Linn*, which seems to include a clear transliteration of the Sanskrit "campaka," suggesting that the two are the same. The flower of this plant is yellow, and it has a rich aroma and elegantly shaped flowers. It is quite suitable for use in Buddhist sacrifices (fig. 67).

Fig. 69 *Gardenia, Lake and Stone* (detail)
Chen Chun
Ink and color on silk
Height 123.8 cm × Width 60.5 cm

Chen Chun made considerable contributions to the development of freehand flower-and-bird paintings after Shen Zhou and Tang Yin (1470–1523). He was greatly appreciated by the literati and scholars of his time.

rugosa roses were brewed into wine, made into cakes, and served in dishes. During the Ming Dynasty, sauce, wine, and smoked tea made with rugosa roses were all widely used. In fact, though the slender branches of the rugosa rose are quite well suited for display in a vase, this use of the flower has not yet been discovered by the Ming Dynasty (fig. 66).

Campaka. The campaka is the traditional name of a flower in the gardenia family originating in China. Several varieties of the flower were planted in the Han Dynasty. In the Tang Dynasty, the gardenia was often planted in the courtyards of ordinary families.

It has a long flowering period and can survive quite long even if it is only placed in water. Its fragrance is strong enough to fill a house. Being so easy to care for, it is frequently found in Chinese homes (figs. 68–69).

Crape myrtle. This deciduous shrub or small tree can grow up to seven meters in height, flowering from June to September. The crape myrtle is graceful and elegant, and its flower colorful. It flowers during summer and autumn, when there are not many flowers blooming. Its flowering period is quite long, resulting in the name "100 days of red" to indicate its flowering season. The crape myrtle is more appropriate for viewing on the branch, rather than in a vase, so it is less common to see the flower plucked and placed in a vase for display (figs. 70–71). It is a very extravagant flower, which later generations regarded as a symbol for civil officials.

Long yellow daylily and tawny daylily. The two flowers form a single, inseparable category. The bright color of the flower brings great joy to viewers, as a smiling face does. Ancient people called these "forgetfulness." Long yellow daylily

Fig. 70 *Crape Myrtle Immersed in Moonlight*
Liu Deliu (Qing Dynasty)
Ink and color on paper
Height 123 cm × Width 43 cm

Liu Deliu was from Wujiang, Jiangsu Province. He drew flowers as a form of self-cultivation, believing that the purpose of life was self-improvement.

Fig. 71 **Crape Myrtle**

Fig. 72 *Hollyhock and Tawny Daylily* (detail)
Jiang Tingxi (Qing Dynasty)
Ink and color on silk
Height 76 cm × Width 39.8 cm
Liaoning Provincial Museum

During the Yongzheng years (1723–1735), Jiang Tingxi from Changshu, Jiangsu Province, served as high official at Ministry of Rites and other roles. He was skilled at flower-and-bird painting and sketching with freestyle strokes. He was one of the important court painters of the mid-Qing Dynasty. Though he tinted his flowers in plain colors, they are vivid and lifelike. He pursued the aesthetic philosophies of the Song Dynasty and the ink style of the Yuan.

can be placed in a vase and used on a table as decoration for appreciation. It is also a noted delicacy (figs. 72–73)

Fragrant Nutmeg. A perennial herb of the Ginger family, this plant grows quite tall. Shaped like a plantain, it has a large leaf, is lanceolate, and light yellow in color. It has medicinal uses, and is slightly aromatic (fig. 74). It was often compared to young girls in Tang poetry.

Fig. 73 **Tawny Daylily**

Fig. 74 **Fragrant Nutmeg**

6. Grade Six

Among the flowers in Grade Six, Tier Four were the magnolia, winter jasmine, hibiscus, royal jasmine, tender willow branches, and sasanqa camellia. Of these, the winter jasmine and royal jasmine are most suitable for arrangement in floral baskets.

Magnolia. The deciduous tree of Magnoliaceae family has flowers ranging from white to pale purple in color. They are large, aromatic flowers with cup-shaped corollas. The flowers open first, followed by leaves appearing on the tree. Its flowering period is roughly ten days. It is among China's famous flowers and trees, and is especially important during early spring in the south (fig. 75). Since the Tang Dynasty, the magnolia has been a symbol of a magnificent hall. It is often planted with the crabapple, symbolizing "a grand hall" (*yutang*, 玉堂) (fig. 76).

The magnolia is not the best spring flower for use in flower arrangements. In a floral arrangement of spring, the first choice are the peony and plum blossom, followed by the camellia, apricot blossom, peach blossom, and pear blossom, with the magnolia rarely being used. When putting lots of flowers together as decorations for ritual use, a couple of branches of magnolia can be used, since their branches are generally thick and their blooms large. For a decoration for ritual suggesting the idea of "a

Fig. 75 **Magnolia**

Fig. 76 *Magnolia, Crabapple, and Orchid*
Sun Kehong (1533–1611)
Ink and color on paper
Height 135cm × Width 59 cm
Palace Museum, Beijing

This classical painting depicts a magnolia and a crabapple. The trunk of the magnolia is straight and elegant, its flowers huge and beautiful. The begonia acts as a foil, looking tender and delicate. Clustered under the magnolia tree is spring orchid, serenely budding, together with magnolia, and crabapple, presenting an image of spring implied by the term *yutangchun* (with the characters sounding in Chinese like magnolia, crabapple and spring respectively).

Fig. 78 *Autumn Scene of Heron and Hibiscus*
Lü Ji (b. 1477)
Ink and color on silk
Height 192.6 cm × Width 111.9 cm
Palace Museum, Taibei

Autumn comes alive under Lü Ji's brush. The painting depicts a triumphant hibiscus bloom, while in the water beneath a lotus withers. On the right side of the scroll a willow tree with thin leaves protrudes abruptly. In this all-withering season, the willow tree remains refreshingly green and strong.

splendid spring in the grand hall," the peony, magnolia, crabapple, and winter jasmine all must be used in abundance. However, judging from the preferences of those more disposed to a secluded life, this sort of ritual arrangement is often too grand and resplendent, inevitably alienating those who view it.

Winter jasmine. These plants of the Jasminum genus are clustered in small shrubs. The flowers are fragrant and their petals are mostly golden yellow with a flush on the outside. Its flowering period is from February to April. Because its flowering season is early, the plant's Chinese name, *yingchun*, indicates its role in welcoming spring. Scholars often give this flower as a gift, as indicated in the verses "pick flowers while they are in blossom, or there will be no blossoms but merely branches." The tender green branches in spring are tough and can be woven into flower baskets or crown, and are often associated with girlish enthusiasm (fig. 77).

Hibiscus. Native to China, this plant of the Malvaceae family grows in deciduous shrubs or arbors of hibiscus plants. Each

branch has a single flower nestling among its leaves (fig. 79). The hibiscus was highly favored in the Tang Dynasty, and was often planted at the water's edge, taking on the meaning of "drawing water before flowers." For this reason, when ancient people painted the hibiscus, it often carried this artistic conception (fig. 78).

Fig. 77 Winter Jasmine

Fig. 79 Hibiscus

Royal jasmine. A small shrub of the Jasminum genus, the same genus as the winter jasmine (fig. 80). It is often mentioned alongside the jasmine, another flowering plant in the same family. These two flowers were often planted together in the Song Dynasty. In the palace of the Southern Song, the jasmine

Fig. 80　Royal Jasmine

was chosen for planting in the courtyard of the summer palace. Hundreds of these two flowers were planted there, filling the palace with their scent when the cool wind blew.

Tender willow branch. It is often used in vase flower arrangements, simply by placing a branch in a vase. It has strong religious symbolism and willow in a plain bottle is a favorite of the Bodhisattva Guanyin, Goddess of Mercy and Sudhada, the disciple at the bottom of her seat.

Sasanqua camellia. This evergreen shrub of the Camellia family is known as *chamei* in Chinese, because of the shape of its flower, which combines characteristics of the camellia and the plum blossom. It is an exquisite-looking plant, colorful, and with a long flowering period—an ideal flower for winter scenes (fig. 81). There are many varieties of the sasanqua camellia, especially horticultural varieties, which can be divided into three groups: sasanqua group, hiemalis group, and oleifera group. The flowers vary greatly, and have a long flowering period. They come in magnificent colors, and both flower and tree are elegantly, beautifully shaped. Most of the branches extend horizontally, creating plump foliage at the tree's top. The amount of flowers on each branch makes it suitable for bonsai appreciation. It is also an ideal flower for both winter and spring arrangements.

7. Grade Seven

Some flowers included among those ranked Grade Seven, Tier Three are Chinese pea shrub, rhododendron molle, wolfberry, garden balsam, Chinese plum, citrus aurantium flower, and azaleas, all of which are very interesting flowers and trees. The rhododendron molle and azalea are actually both plants from the Rhododendron genus, while the wolfberry and the citrus aurantium are types used in Chinese herbal medicine. How these plants were used for ornamental purposes during the Ming Dynasty is an area that still remains to be studied. Chinese pea shrub was good for floral arrangements, while the garden balsam was generally used by unmarried ladies to color their nails. Chinese plum was still acceptable for use in floral arrangements.

Chinese pea shrub. This deciduous shrub belongs to the Leguminous family. In the wild, they mostly grow on hillsides, at the edge or in crevices with loose soil. They require good light and are drought- and cold-tolerant, making them suitable for relatively arid conditions. They are highly adaptable plants. In late spring and early summer, the flowers bloom with golden butterfly-shaped petals. When the flowers are in bloom, they fill the trees, creating a charming scene. The

Fig. 81　**Sasanqua Camellia**

Fig. 82 Chinese Pea Shrub

Fig. 84 Wolfberry

Fig. 83 Rhododendron Molle

plants are suitable for bonsai, and also for situating as part of a scene. When used in a floral arrangement, a bundle of its twigs should be placed in a vase. It has luxuriant green leaves and bright flowers, with contrast between the greens and yellows of the plant. Its appearance is lush, warm, and impressive (fig. 82).

Rhododendron molle. This flower is a deciduous shrub of the Azalea family with a funnel-shaped corolla 4.5 cm long. It is a golden yellow flower with deep red spots on the inside and a light layer of villi on the outside. It flowers from March to May, and bears fruit from July to August (fig. 83).

Wolfberry. The wolfberry is a deciduous shrub, and a rare material most commonly used in Chinese medicine (fig. 84). It is also known as an ornamental plant, and during the Tang Dynasty, it was once believed to be a magical medicine. It was often planted beside wells or grown on a trellis. The spirit of all the springs lingered in it, and it was thought to increase longevity. Though by the Ming Dynasty it was no longer popular, if there was a suitable place to plant it, it could certainly be used in a garden. Poets often reveled in eating these berries, but it is difficult to find any record of their use in vase flower arrangements.

Garden balsam. This plant, a member of the Impatiens genus, has a crane-like top and the coloring of a phoenix. It stands beautifully, creating a charming view. It was commonly found in courtyards and was suitable for planting, bouquets, and potted plants. Its cut flowers could also be kept just in water (fig. 85). Its main use was for coloring the nails. The garden balsam is a girl's boudoir flower and when it blooms in the summer, it has a faint aroma which is thick and sweet. It was most commonly used as adornment for beautiful ladies (fig. 86).

Fig. 86 *Chrysanthemum and Garden Balsam*

Dong Qi (Qing Dynasty)
Ink and color on silk
Height 119 cm × Width 43.5 cm

Dong Qi often came and went between Jiaxing and Huzhou. His landscape, figure, flower-and-bird, and insect paintings are all subtle, paying careful attention to the "character" and "personality" of self-cultivation.

Fig. 85 Garden Balsam

Fig. 87   Chinese Plum

Fig. 89   Citrus Aurantium Flower

Chinese plum. This refers to the ornamental species of the Prunus. There are many varieties of Chinese plum, and the tree has many white, elegant flowers. The Chinese plum flower is excellent for display in a vase, but was silently forgotten in the shadows of more popular flowers such as the peach, apricot, and pear blossoms (fig. 87).

Citrus aurantium flower. Its fruit is sour, but when dried, is often used for medicinal purposes. It has the effect of expanding the qi and reducing swelling. In the Jiangnan area, there is a tradition of visiting gardens to view the citrus aurantium blossom. The flowers bloom at the end of spring and have arich fragrance. Even though they are not as bright as the peach and plum blossoms, the scene of citrus aurantium flowers filling the whole garden with their rich fragrance at the end of spring presents a different kind of atmosphere, so it was greatly appreciated by poets (fig. 89). Many people appreciate the

flower, but it is not so frequently used. The citrus aurantium tree has tough wood, and its branches are thorny and not easily broken, unlike the peach and Prunus, which can be easily cut and arranged. Citrus aurantium blossoms are quite idyllic, but all of its flowers are pale, so a single branch does not make for a very nice arrangement.

Azalea. The azalea is very popular in modern flower arrangements (fig. 88). In ancient times, the azalea had quite plaintive symbolic associates, so the flowers were not seen as sufficiently festive. As a result, they were not often used in arrangements for decoration on the desk. After it was introduced into Europe, it became very popular among Europeans, and horticulturalists there became obsessed with cultivating hybrid varieties.

8. Grade Eight

Hollyhock. This herbaceous plant of the Malvaceae family was called *shukui* in ancient times because it originated in Sichuan. The hollyhock is a tall plant, up to two meters in height, flowering in early summer, with a flowering period that lasts from June to August. It is beautifully colored in purple, pink, red, and white varieties, making it a lovely plant for viewing (see fig. 90 on page 66). This herbaceous flower was widely cultivated in Jiangnan gardens during the Ming Dynasty and became widely loved by painters (see fig. 91 on page 66). This is a

Fig. 88   Azalea

classical flower that is largely ignored in modern times, being rarely used in plantings today.

Hosta plantaginea. It is a perennial herbaceous flower of Liliaceae family, named in Chinese for its jade-like buds, which resemble a hairpin. Its flowers are white, tubular, funnel-shaped, and aromatic. Flowering from July to September, it is famed in Chinese tradition for its fragrant blooms (fig. 92). As a shade-loving plant, it can be used as ground cover under other trees in a garden, or be planted on the north side of a rock garden or a building. It can also be displayed as a potted plant for ornamentation or as cut flowers. It is an indispensable flower in a

Fig. 91 *Hollyhock, Rockery and Butterfly*
Dai Jin (1388–1462)
Ink and color on paper
Height 115 cm × Width 39.6 cm
Palace Museum, Beijing

This painting depicts a blooming hollyhock, with two fluttering butterflies. The lower part of the picture shows the rough surface and unevenness of the lake rock, creating a sharp contrast with the flowers and insects. The brushstrokes are fine, and the colors are beautifully composed.

Fig. 90 **Hollyhock**

night garden because it opens after dark, when it exudes a rich aroma.

Cockscomb. This herbaceous plant belongs to the Amaranthaceae family. It is often planted on hillsides and roadsides, and is commonly used in garden greening. The flower can be included in this as well, in that it has been used since the Song Dynasty for the special purpose of worshipping ancestors. The custom of using cockscomb in ancestor worship rituals continued into the Ming and Qing dynasties (figs. 93–94).

China pink. A perennial herb of the Dianthus genus, the China pink is commonly used in modern gardening. Low in height, its stalks are like bamboo, and it has green leaves. Its natural flowering period is from May to

Fig. 92 **Hosta Plantaginea**

Fig. 93 *Portrait of Confucius: Prayer at the Niqui Hill* (detail)

Qiu Ying
Height approx. 60 cm × Width approx. 40 cm

According to the *Historical Records* (*Shi Ji*), Confucius' (551–479 BC) parents "prayed at the Niqiu hill and begot Confucius." This painting depicts this story. The interesting thing about this painting is that Confucius' mother, who lived in the late Spring and Autumn Period, is carrying a type of flower stand peculiar to the Ming Dynasty, on which there is a blue porcelain Ming vase with two purple cockscomb flowers in it.

Fig. 94
Cockscomb

September, lasting from late spring to mid-autumn. Greenhouse potted varieties can flower throughout the four seasons

Fig. 95 China Pink

(fig. 95). It is ideal for flower arrangements, due to its luxuriant flowers and long viewing period. Its flowers are white, pink, red, lavender, yellow, or blue. It is a flower with great variety, and well suited for vase flower arrangements.

Malus pumila flower. This species of Chinese apple has been cultivated in China for more than 2,000 years. A small tree of the Rosaceae family, it boasts beautiful blooms during its April to May flowering season. It resembles the kaido crabapple. Its fruit-bearing period is from August to September. The fruit is sweet and attracts many birds, giving the plant its Chinese name (fig. 96).

Sunset muskmallow. This plant refers to a herb of the Malvaceae family. It grows one to two meters tall and has large leaves. Its flowering period is from June to August. Its flowers are large and brightly colored, and it is a plant that has long been used in gardens (fig. 97).

9. Grade Nine

Lychnis coronata. Flowering from June to July, it is a perennial herb of the Caryophyllaceae family. It has bright, colorful flowers and is highly adaptable. It is best planted in open forests, but is also suitable for flower beds and flower arrangements (fig. 98).

Brilliant campion. This perennial herb of the Caryophyllaceae family is also known as the large flowered campion. It has ovate oblate or ovate lanceolate leaves with a sharp apex, both sides of which are covered in a light fuzz. Its flowers, mostly red and yellow, bloom in June and July (fig. 99).

Lesser galangal flower. Often used for medicinal purposes, the lesser galangal is also a fine flower for viewing. A member of the Ginger family, it is a perennial herb with a cone-shaped raceme and a funnel-shaped corolla. It is white or light red, and flowers from April to October. Its dry rhizome is an important ingredient in Chinese medicine, useful for its warming effect on the stomach and its ability to stop vomiting and dispel cold and pain (fig. 100). The alpinia zerumbet, commonly known as shell ginger, has beautiful leaves, and flowers from May to July. Its elegant flowers are particularly attractive, making it a renowned ornamental flower.

Fig. 96 **Malus Pumila Flower**

Fig. 97 **Sunset Muskmallow**

Fig. 98　Lychnis Coronata

Fig. 100　Lesser Galangal Flower

Fig. 99　Brilliant Campion

Fig. 101　Dianthus

Dianthus. This is a herb of the same genus as the carnation. Its branches are leafy and resplendently verdant. Single flowers grow on each branch, with single or double petals. It comes in light red, red light purple, purple, white, multicolored, and other varieties. It flowers from May to October (fig. 101).

Morning glory. This annual herb of the Convolvulaceae family grows as a sprawling plant with slender stems of about three to four meters in length. Its corolla is horn-shaped, and its flowers bright and beautiful. They are excellent ornamental plants for the garden, and also useful in hedges. Its popular name in Chinese is "working lady," referring to its pre-dawn bright bloom on the vines growing up a lattice.

Chaenomeles cathayensis. This deciduous shrub or small tree of Rosaceae family, flowering from March to May and bearing fruit from September to October. It flowers before its leaves appear, with large flowers, mostly double blooms. It comes in

a range of colors including orange, dark red, pure white, and light green. The flowering period is long, and the plant is resistant to pruning. It makes an excellent ornamental flower (see fig. 102 on page 70). The flower is mentioned in the ancient poetry collection *Book of Songs* (*Shi Jing*). Its colorful, elegant flowers can be planted along the garden walls, at the edge of groves, and in other similar locations. Its flowers can be appreciated in spring, and its fruit in autumn. It is an exceptional species for garden scenery (see fig. 104 on page 70).

Lophatherum. This plant is more a Chinese herb than a flower for arrangement. It is a perennial herbaceous plant that grows mainly in the shade of a mountain or under thick foliage in parts of Jiangnan. It is commonly used in Chinese herbal medicine (see fig. 103 on page 70). When included in a flower arrangement, it should be used in combination with other flowers, capitalizing on its green, elegant bamboo-like leaves.

Fig. 102 **Chaenomeles Cathayensis**

Fig. 104 ***Antique and Flower*** (detail)
Huang Shiling
Ink and color on paper
Height 102.5 cm × Width 32 cm

In this painting, a bright red chaenomeles cathayensis is placed in a bronze vase, leaning to one side. The flowers have five petals, and gold stamen. It flowers before its leaves appear, so in this painting, the leaves have been omitted.

Fig. 103 **Lophatherum**

Plants in the Caryophyllaceae Family

The lychnis coronata and brilliant campion are all plants in the Caryophyllaceae family (fig. 105). This family of plants is characterized by beautiful blooms and long flowering periods, which results in a good ornamental effect. As an exceptional flowering plant, it is good for cut flower arrangements. Carnations are likewise a part of this family. They are welcome additions in modern flower arrangements, and are used widely for this purpose throughout the world.

There are many varieties of this family, with about 2,200 species in 86 genera. Worldwide, there are about 600 species of the Dianthus genus, widely distributed throughout Europe, Asia, and Africa, particularly in the Mediterranean region.

China pink have a long history of cultivation in China. The Tang Dynasty poet Sikong Shu writes of this flower in his poem *The China Pink in the Yunyang Temple*. In the poem, the flower blooms among the grass, as bright as a butterfly in red and white tones. The flower grows in red or white, and its white variety is whiter than a white butterfly, while the red is redder than a pomegranate flower. It has a long flowering period, lasting from spring until autumn.

China pink is a perennial flower. Gao Lian writes, "Its roots remain, so the old flowers can still be seen." This means that even if the stem and leaves wither, the roots remain, and when the following spring comes, they will sprout once again, and will again flower. In modern horticultural terms, this is called a perennial flower.

Fig. 105 *Vase Flower Arrangement*
Li Shan (1686–1762)
Ink and color on paper
Height 24.5 cm × Width 35.5 cm

Li Shan was one of the Eight Eccentric Artists of Yangzhou. In the 50th year of Kangxi's reign, he turned a successful candidate in the imperial examinations at the provincial level and became a court painter, but he was later excluded because he was unwilling to be constrained by the "orthodox" style of painting.

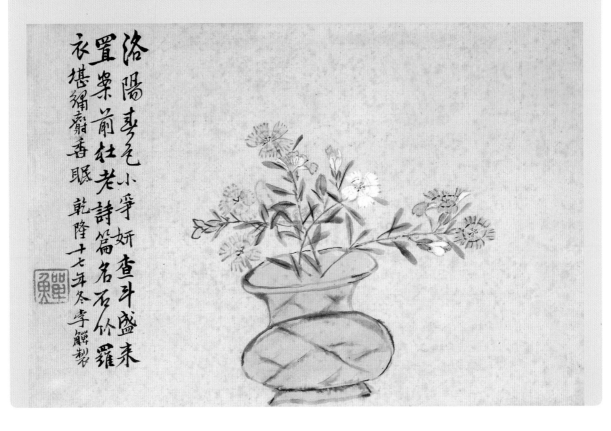

與最高枝唐寅
婦娥愛子桂花折
鶴天秀捲繡権自是
廣寒宮闕舊遊時鸞

Fig. 106 *Chang'e Holding Scented Osmanthus* (detail)

Anonymous (Ming Dynasty), after Tang Yin
Ink and color on Paper
Height 136.2 cm × Width 58.7 cm
The Metropolitan Museum of Art, New York

In the painting, Chang'e is holding a stalk of scented osmanthus. Her garments are flowing, while her expression and form are gentle and soft. A woman of such beauty is always closely related to flowers.

CHAPTER 3
PICKING FLOWERS

THE ORIGINAL TEXT

Flower picking definitely must be done in the family garden or an adjacent flower garden. At dawn, when the blooms are wet with dew, flowers that have only half opened should be selected for cutting, which will preserve the fragrance of the flowers even if they are cut several days in a row. If it is a sunny day, the scent will not be preserved after the dew dries, nor will the color be bright, and the flower will wither after just a day or two.

When picking flowers, the branch must first be selected. It is best to choose one with a heap of flowers on the upper limb, while its lower limb is very thin, or choose a branch with flowers growing high on one side and flowers growing low on the opposite side, or pick two branches interconnected with abundant flowers causing the branches to droop and bend. Alternatively, one can take a straight stem from the middle, with a cluster of flowers at the top of the stem and thick leaves at the lower part which cover the mouth of the vase. In selecting the branch and flowers, it is important to consider the posture and the density of the branch. Each branch has a unique look, allowing the artist's brush to capture the full expression of each floral scene. Only when this effect is duplicated in an arrangement can it be said to posses a sort of natural charm. If a plant's branches are straight and its flowers full and unruly, it is not well suited for a vase flower arrangement (fig. 107).

Whether herbaceous or ligneous, flowers can be harvested for arrangement in a vase. There are two ways to give proper attention to the removal of a flowering branch, plucking by hand (fig. 106) or cutting with a tool. The former is more suitable for tender twigs, while the latter is used for sturdier branches. Those who take an interest in flowers need to understand this. It is easier to cut hardier branches, while herbaceous flowers are the hardiest to pluck. Unless one studies intensively the sketches of famous artists, it will be hard to attain refinement.

Fig. 107 *A Painting of Malus Pumila Flower* (detail)
Anonymous (Southern Song Dynasty), after Zhao Chang (Northern Song Dynasty)
Ink and color on silk
Height 23.5 cm × Width 25.2 cm
Hatakeyama Memorial Museum of Fine Art, Tokyo

Zhao Chang was active during the early Northern Song Dynasty. He was skilled in flower-and-bird painting, but mostly painted plucked flowers. This painting had refined brush strokes and light, elegant colors. His work was hailed as famous among Song Dynasty flower-and-bird paintings.

To the literati, flower arrangement was a refined activity. Any flower, whether herbaceous or ligneous can be picked and used in a vase arrangement. The placement of the branches was to be based on the same principles of composition as an artist's painting. Each branch has a unique look and form, giving it a natural charm (fig. 108).

1. Timing of the Selection: Preservation

The ancients used daylight to judge the time of day, and flowers do the same. At dawn, dew is found on the flowers, making it easier to preserve them. If one waits until the sun is high, the best time for plucking the flowers will have passed, and it will be more difficult to keep them fresh.

Today, the rugosa rose plantation in Shaanxi Province still retains the tradition of plucking rugosa roses in the early morning. Flower pickers rise at three in the morning, entering the garden by moonlight. After the nourishing night dew falls, the flower quietly comes into full bloom, emitting a beautiful aroma. It is this precise point that is most ideal for plucking the best flower. Because of the heavy dew on the branches, the flower collectors wear rain boots and raincoats to avoid being soaked in dew.

2. Branch Selection and Flower Painting

In selecting a branch, Zhang Qiande suggests choosing one that most closely resembles the way flowers are depicted by painters, which is to say the way the branch bends, high or low, the density and spacing, all depict different moods. Choosing a branch of flowers is a particular skill, requiring a painter's sensibilities if one is to obtain the desired effect from the flowering branches. Herbaceous and ligneous flowers are plucked using different methods, with herbaceous flowers being the more difficult to pluck.

This selection is meant to be a commentary on painting's influence on floral arrangements, rather than a discussion of floral arrangements per se. The flowers in paintings have an ancient feel, elegant and tranquil. The

Fig. 108 *Flowers on Branches on Four Screens*

Ma Jiatong (Qing Dynasty)
Ink and color on silk
Height 133 cm × Width 32 cm × 4

Ma Jiatong, a native of Tianjin, was known as one of the Four Painters of Tianjin during the Tongzhi (1862–1874) and Guangxu (1875–1908) years in the Qing Dynasty. He was skilled at paintings of landscapes and flowers and his copy of ancient paintings was so great that they were often taken as the original.

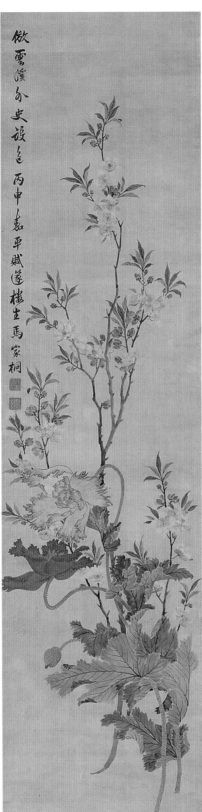

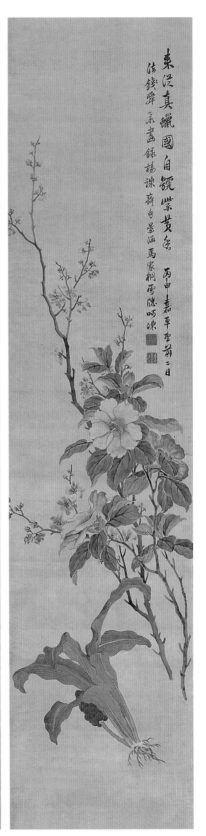

flowers that bloom in the vase are bright, fragrant, and full of vitality. When depicted in a painting, flowers are always perfectly matched to the vase in which they are arranged.

Flower depiction is an expression of Chinese flower-and-bird paintings. The painting of flowers does not have the sketching of an entire plant, but only of one or a few specially selected branches or twigs, giving the form its name *zhezhi* in ancient Chinese. Traditional flower-and-bird paintings offer a concise expression of flowers in their natural environment. They are a reflection both of the natural and the poetic world.

From the mid to late Tang Dynasty, the painter Bian Luan had already begun to include floral arrangements in the composition of his paintings. During the Five Dynasties period, the arrangement and drawing method had become more common. In the Song Dynasty, painting of flowering branches was popular, with vivid, natural representations

reflecting the aesthetic conception typical of the Song Dynasty (fig. 109).

The literati of the Song Dynasty loved flowers, and painters of that era were likewise eager to paint them. They were meticulous in every aspect of depicting the natural world. In the middle of the Northern Song Dynasty, Su Shi was at the center of the circle of literary scholars and painters, alongside painter and poet Wen Tong (1018–1079), painter Li Gonglin (1049–1106), painter and calligrapher Mi Fu (1051–1107), and other literati and scholars who created paintings, many of which had inward expression at their core. The themes of such pieces were often centered around landscapes, trees, or flowers as a means of expressing the feelings of the gentry.

During the Ming Dynasty, painters of the Wumen School were skilled at flower-and-bird paintings. These painters, all from Wu County (present day Suzhou, Jiangsu Province), were represented by notable figures such as Shen Zhou, Wen Zhengming, Tang Yin, Qiu Ying, Zhang Hong (1580–1649), and others. Among them, Shen Zhou is known for his concise, vigorous strokes. Wen Zhengming studied under Shen Zhou, absorbing the paintings of Zhao Mengfu and Wang Meng (1308 or 1301–1385), and was known for his meticulous

Fig. 109 *Crape Myrtle* (detail)
Wei Sheng (Southern Song Dynasty)
Ink and color on silk
Height 23.8 cm × Width 25.3 cm
Palace Museum, Taibei

Wei Sheng captured an outstanding vision of a crape myrtle in a summer garden then, taking up his brush, condensed the view onto the silk for all eternity. The crape myrtle extends from bottom left, its stamen, petals, and full bud successfully capturing the characteristics of the crape myrtle.

workmanship and gentle, elegant, fine strokes. After Shen Zhou and Wen Zhengming, those who pursued freehand painting of flowers included disciples such as Chen Chun, Lu Zhi, and Sun Ai, who achieved great success. Chen Chun and Lu Zhi (fig. 110) was best at floral paintings. Since Zhang Qiande's family were keen collectors of paintings and calligraphies, he was naturally close to the members of the Wumen School, and he was greatly influenced by them. In plucking herbaceous flowers, there is no

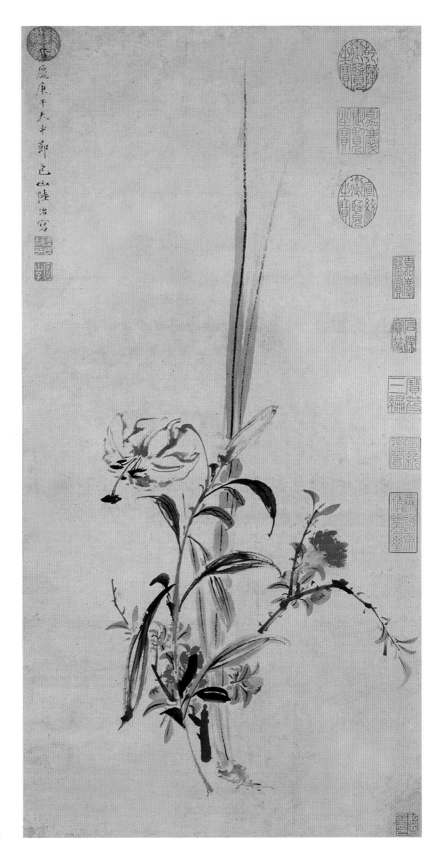

Fig. 110 *Small Scene of Pomegranate Flower* (detail)

Lu Zhi
Ink and color on paper
Height 65.3 cm × Width 33.3 cm
Palace Museum, Taibei

The composition of this piece is simple, tidy, and understated in its elegance. The three plants in the picture stand gracefully side by side, creating natural interest. The artist uses cinnabar for pomegranate, cyanine for calami, and ink for lilies, with ink outlining the leaves, presumably to capture the flowers in the image, twisting them in a graceful pattern recalling the ideal of Zhang Qiande.

The Beauty Picking Flowers in Chinese Paintings

Since the Tang Dynasty, it was customary for the beautiful women of the court to engage in flower arrangement and hair decoration. This activity remained quite popular throughout the Five Dynasties and Song Dynasty periods. For Ming Dynasty painters in Jiangnan, such scenes came to be among their favorite subjects for paintings. Such paintings depicted the exquisite, extravagant lifestyle of the court. They satisfied the common people's desire for novelty, as well as for a peek into the lives of the nobility, and expanded the stunning beauty and lively sweetness of the court.

Qiu Ying's *Royal Makeup in the Morning* (fig. 111) is a Ming Dynasty depiction of a scene of the morning dressing of Concubine Yang (Yang Yuhuan, 719–756). The Tang Dynasty palace seen in the painting is magnificent, with the ladies of the court gathered there playing harps. Amidst the gentle music, two serving women stand by to dress Concubine Yang. Also shown in the painting is a female official leading two young maidens through the garden to collect flowers for Concubine Yang's hair decoration. It is late spring, as seen from crabapples in full bloom, which the maidens are plucking. It is a lively, interesting scene. Qiu Ying was skilled at figure painting, particularly those depicting courtly ladies. His figures are accurate, his images beautiful,

Fig. 111 *"Royal Makeup in the Morning"* from the *Figure Story Album* (detail)
Qiu Ying
Ink and color on silk
Height 41.4 cm × Width 33.8 cm
Palace Museum, Beijing

In the royal morning makeup, a female officer leads young maids into a garden to pick flowers for the royal lady to pin her hair. It is a spring day, with beautiful, tender crabapples opening in the garden. The maids pick crabapples from the branches with their bare hands.

and his lines smooth. His paintings present a model of female beauty in the Ming Dynasty.

substitute for the refinement that comes from familiarity with the floral paintings of the masters.

Plucking flowers depicted in ancient poetry were also very elegant. Lu Kai, a politician of the Northern and Southern Dynasties era, perhaps captures it best in his poem *To Fan Ye*, "Meeting a messenger while picking flowers, I sent them to my friend in Chang'an; with nothing much in Jiangnan, all I can offer is a branch of spring." In this poem, it is

plum blossom season, and the poet picks a branch. Holding the flower as he walks, he happens to meet a messenger; so he sends the branch with the messenger to a friend who is stationed far away in Chang'an. Sending a plum blossom across thousands of miles was a particularly elegant gesture. In the poetry of the Tang Dynasty, flowers are the most popular imagery. From this, it is evident that flower arranging was an elegant pastime of the young people in the upper class of that time.

CHAPTER 4
FLORAL ARRANGEMENT

THE ORIGINAL TEXT

Upon cutting a branch of flowers, it must quickly be placed in a vase and the mouth tightly plugged. It is important that air from inside the vase not be allowed to escape, which will allow the flower to be kept for several days.

Generally, floral arrangements need to be harmonious with the vase, sitting slightly higher than it (fig. 112). If the vase is roughly one *chi* (roughly 31.1 cm) high, the flowering branch should be one *chi* and three to four *cun* (roughly 40–43 cm) high. If the vase is six or seven *cun* (roughly 18.66–21.77 cm) high, the flowering branch should be about eight to nine *cun* (roughly 24–28 cm) above the mouth of the vase. It is a taboo to situate it too high, as that will likely topple the vase.

At the same time, it is equally undesirable to have it situated too low, as it loses its elegance.

It is best to use relatively small vases for flower arrangements. Flowering branches should be thin, small and uncomplicated. If a single branch is to be arranged, it is important to select one that is unique and quaint, with an oblique curve to the branch. If two branches are to be used, they need to be of different heights, so as to create variety, just as is seen in natural plants. Alternatively, the two branches can be placed facing one another, with the first forming a cluster and bound with string before it is placed inside the vase.

Though it is a taboo for flower arrangements to be too complicated, it is a greater taboo for branches to be thinner than the vase. Sloping flowering branches must be taken and spread out on either side of a small vase to be considered presentable. Only one or two types of flowers should be used in a single arrangement, to prevent it from becoming too overbearing or messy. Use of too many types of flowers will be annoying, except with autumn blossoms.

Fig. 112 *Painting of Autumn Flowers in a Gallbladder-Shaped Pot* (detail)
Anonymous (Song Dynasty)
Ink and color on silk
Height 26.5 cm × Width 27.5 cm
Palace Museum, Beijing

This painting has a blue glazed flask on a stand, with chrysanthemums in it. The flowers and leaves are depicted in a natural and delicate way, in soft, gentle colors.

THE MODERN READER

In speaking of arranging flowers, Gao Lian remarked, "The activities of flower arrangement and painting reflect the true interest of the doer, which could not be accomplished by the hands of the servant." Both flower arrangement and painting are different from ordinary activities. If one undertakes a project of this sort, he cannot simply tell a servant to complete the task for him, or it will become uninteresting (fig. 113). Floral arrangement requires one to match flower and vase, dictating casualness in arrangements for big vases instead of over-modification, and slim and uncomplicated flower arrangements for small vases.

Fig. 113 *Apprentice*
Chen Hongshou
Ink and color on silk
Height 90.4 cm × Width 46 cm
California Museum of Art Collection, USA

This painting depicts a scene of vase flower arranging after a flower has been plucked. In the painting, a nobleman sits at a table beside a rockery from Lake Tai. There are paintings, calligraphies, and a teapot on the table. Two female students sit on stools, one looking at the *Bamboo and Rocks* scroll, and the other arranging flowers in a vase. It is a long-necked bronze vase with a long branch of plum blossom. From this, it is evident that the flower arrangement is not being made as part of a "boudoir pastime," but is work descended from the literati. To study flower arrangement one needed a period of apprenticeship.

1. Preservation

After arranging the flower branch, it must be placed in a vase, a process that must be completed in a short period of time. The air must not be allowed to escape from the vase, in order to ensure that the flowers can be enjoyed for a period of several days.

Even in the ancient rules of flower arrangement, such arguments are not always supported. Because not all flower containers have small mouths, many vessels are left open, but with such large openings, the flowers will not be kept alive very long. For instance, a bronze *gu* used to contain flowers will have a large mouth, so the air cannot be kept in. Even so, ancient scholars were full of praise for such vessels, though this particular aspect could not be helped.

2. Composition of a Flower Arrangement

Floral composition must focus on the three-dimensional. It is important to consider the proportions of the materials, both flowers and vessels, in order to determine the aesthetics of the overall design (fig. 114). Here, Zhang Qiande provides what he considers the best ratios.

Modern floral arrangements likewise give attention to proportions. Before the flowers are arranged, their size must first be determined. The golden section is used as a rule of thumb, meaning that the proportion of vase height to flower to total height should be 3:5:8. Conventionally, the height of the first main branch of the flower arrangement should not exceed twice the height of the vase, and the height of the second main branch should be two-thirds that of the first, while the height of the third main branch is half that of the second. When this arrangement is followed, the second and third main branches play a balancing role in the composition. The

Fig. 114 *Flowers in Decoration for Appreciation* (detail)
Giuseppe Castiglione
Ink and color on paper
Height 73.5 cm × Width 37 cm
Castiglione's floral work impresses with its eye-catching color and vivid texture. In his paintings, though traces of Western painting techniques are evident, he captures the atmosphere of a traditional Chinese flower-and-bird painting.

number of flowering branches that can be used is not limited, but the size and proportionate height must be coordinated. The drawback of applying this method is that, though the overall shape is quite satisfactory and there is no fault to be found with it, it lacks personality.

People in ancient China saw floral arrangement purely as a form of entertainment for the gentrified class. The floral materials themselves were almost completely unadorned when used in arrangements. They were merely plucked at random and placed in vases in a very relaxed manner.

3. Small Vase Flower Arrangement

Flowers used as decoration for appreciation in small vases were the focus of careful study among the literati. Zhang Qiande believed that a small vase should not be overly complicated, and that one or two types of flowers could be placed in it. If a single flowering branch is placed in the vase, it is important to carefully select the branch, so as to achieve a "stand-alone" effect. If two branches are used, it is important to pay attention to their relationship with each other, creating a harmonious feel.

In general, the plum blossom is usually placed as a single branch, which is called a "single plum blossom cutting." The plum blossom branches should slope downward, with a sloping feel to the slender branches. If the vase is too small, it will not create a harmonious view. Gao Lian said, "It would be more satisfying to cut a large branch of plum blossom for decoration." This is another way of saying that it is ideal—or even necessary—to be a little wild in arranging plum blossoms for decoration when cutting a large branch.

4. Autumn Flower Arrangements

In the section on autumn flowers, there is a note entitled "autumn chrysanthemum," which has yet to be identified. Its literal meaning, "autumn flowers," seems to refer to flowers that bloom in the autumn, which includes not just chrysanthemums (fig. 115), but also osmanthus and hibiscus.

The late Ming Dynasty artist Chen Hongshou offered an excellent demonstration of how autumn flowers ought to be placed. The painting *Vase flower Arrangement* is an example of freestyle flower arrangement. In the golden season, after an autumn rain, the chrysanthemum blooms and a few herbaceous flowers sprout, and these can be placed together in a vase to compose a single autumn scene. Such arrangements are not only handed down in painting masterpieces, but are also classic works of Ming Dynasty floral arrangement. The two vases of flowers are naturally smooth and very original. A long branch is placed in a large vase, its red leaves still covered in dew, and accompanied by autumn herbaceous flowers. They appear to be cockscombs, with the leaves carefully drawn. There are some dry spots on the leaves, and the flowers are not quite perfect, embodying more of a mottled beauty. The highlights of the vase are two wild chrysanthemums and small white flowers in clusters, a very lively, attractive scene. Next to the vase is a cluster of wild chrysanthemums mingled with a pair of wild roses, arranged in a bit of a jumble that creates a playful feeling

Fig. 115 *Potted Chrysanthemum Scene* (detail)
Shen Zhou
Ink and color on paper
Height 23.4 cm × Width 334.6 cm
Liaoning Provincial Museum

This is a small garden landscape. There are varied trees around a thatched pavilion, surrounded by a curved fenced courtyard. In the courtyard are a number of blooming potted chrysanthemums. Three people are drinking in the pavilion, and a boy servant stands nearby, holding a pot. The scene creates an autumnal atmosphere.

China and Japanese Ikenobo School of Ikebana

There is a deep relationship between Japanese floral arrangement (Ikebana) and Buddhism. Ikenobo is Japan's oldest school of floral arrangement, having celebrated its 550th anniversary in 2012. During the Sui Dynasty (581–618), Japan's ambassador arrived in China and converted to Buddhism. When he returned to Japan, he took the art of Buddhist floral arrangement with him. There were many monks at the Rokkaku-dō, officially named Chōhō-ji (a Buddhist temple) in Kyoto, many of whom specialized in upright flower arranging. In its poolside cottages, there were numerous examples of superb floral art to be admired. This led to the Japanese name of the art form, Ikenobo, meaning "poolside."

Compared to the vase floral arrangements discussed by Zhang Qiande in the Ming Dynasty, Ikenobo pays more attention to artificial, artistic effects. In the course of arranging, the natural flowers and plants are refined and sublimated, generating a particular interpretation of certain beliefs or mindsets through the artistry. The Ikenobo artists liked to increase the proportion of the materials in the overall shape of the arrangement, with ratios far exceeding the golden section, making the flowers look especially slender. An extended main branch heightens the whole arrangement while decreasing the center of gravity, creating a unique effect. These artists further polished every detail of the arrangement in very deliberate ways, striving to perfect each leaf without leaving a single defect. The grass and leaves plucked off the branch would never show, and wild chrysanthemums would not shrink into a ball. Not a single extra leaf would be left on the flowering branches (figs. 116–119).

Figs. 116–119 Taken from *View of a Hundred Ikenobo Flowers*. These peonies and magnolias are kept in flat-bodied wicker flower pots. Beautiful and elegant, the pots help to mute the resplendence of the peonies and the magnolias (the two on the left). These two delicate, beautiful herbaceous flowers arrangements display long, green leaves, which raise the overall height of the vase, while the herbaceous flowers stabilizes the center of gravity. Though the shape of the piece can be a bit erratic, the use of a tripod-type device makes for a solid visual effect (the two on the right).

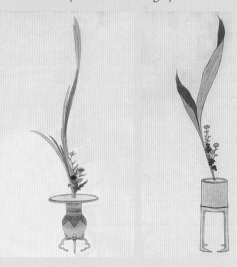

(see fig. 120 on page 84).
An arrangement of this sort is willfully random, natural, and smooth, creating a natural sense of carving that suggests an air of "autumn-struck." This can also be seen as a major difference with Japanese styles of flower arrangements. That form of more exquisitely beautiful works has a quality of weakness, aesthetically, while a more natural beauty will have a more pleasingly robust effect.

Fig. 120 *Vase Flower Arrangement*

Chen Hongshou
Ink and color on silk
Height 274 cm ×
Width 122.5 cm
The British Museum, London

In a large vase, the leaves of a long branch grow, bright red, and the leaves of two herbaceous flowers (like cockscomb) are dragged down, with withered spots on the leaves. Two white wild chrysanthemums are clustered together in the vase, very beautiful. Alongside the vase is a small one in which a cluster of wild chrysanthemums is mingled with a pair of wild roses, an odd match overflowing with joy of life.

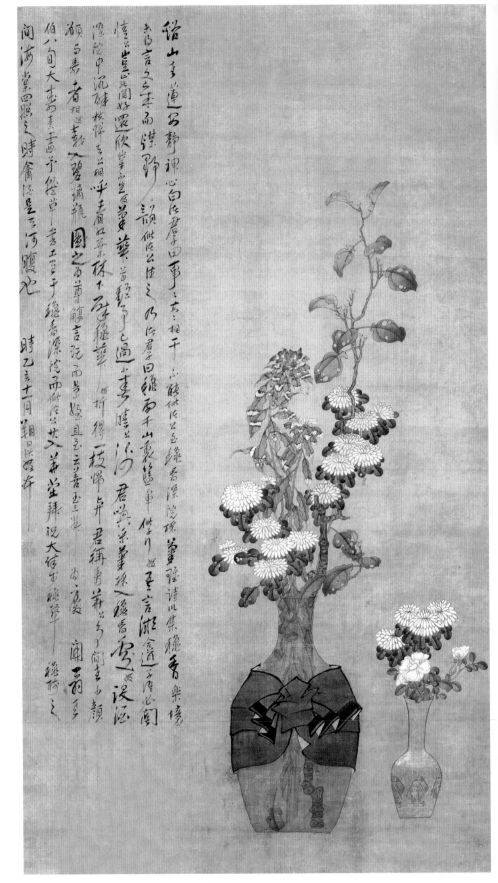

CHAPTER 5
CULTIVATION

THE ORIGINAL TEXT

All flowers and plants grow through nourishment from the rain, so it is suitable to use "water from the sky" (i.e., rainwater) in vase floral arrangements, which allows plants to continue being nourished by the rain. It is even more suitable to use honey water to nourish a flower in a vase, or boiled water for its cultivation. In appreciating flowers, it is necessary to apply appropriate rules of cultivation according to the flower or plant's characteristics. Since it is preferable to use rainwater for flowers kept in a vase, it is necessary to find appropriate means for collecting rainwater. If no way can be found to do so, the water from clear rivers or lakes can be used. Well water is too salty; if it is used for nourishing plants, the flowers will not grow, so it should not be used. The water used for vase flower arrangements generally has trace amounts of toxins, so it is necessary to change the water daily, allowing the branches to flower longer. If the water is not changed for two or three days, the flower will wilt. Each night, the vase flower arrangements should be placed in a sheltered, open air place, which will enable them to be enjoyed for days. In this way, nature and humans interact, and it is necessary for human action to conform to the amazing laws of nature.

Water from the Sky (*Tianshui*)

The ancients referred to rainwater, snowfall, and so forth as "the wellsprings of heaven" (*tianquan*). This sort of water is not only useful for marking seasons in solar terms, but is also used for brewing tea, an area of great expertise among ancient scholars.

When referring to it as "the wellsprings of heaven" in *Treatise on Superfluous Things*, Wen Zhenheng analyzes *tianquan* in this way, "Of the waters from the wellspring of heaven, autumn waters are best, followed by rainy season water. Autumn water is pure and clear, while rainy season water is clear and sweet. Spring water is better than winter water, being covered with gentle wind and rain. Summer rain is least suitable, because of the wind and thunder dragons, which can harm humans. The snow is essential for grains, and for brewing tea, it is most tranquil, but newly fallen snow is rustic and not as good as the slightly aged. Cloth should be used to hold the water in the center of the courtyard, rather than let it flow across the eave."

The same principles are true for both brewing tea and arranging flowers. However, close attention must be paid and careful study made in order to master these principles.

Fig. 121 *Decoration for Appreciation on the First Day of the Lunar Calendar*

Hu Gongshou (Qing Dynasty)

In this patining, there are wintersweets and green feathers in the tall vase and peonies, and narcissus in the short one. According to the title given by the artist, the painting was drawn as a prayer, for "the eternal wealth of the gods."

Zhang Qiande believed "water from the sky" was the best water for use in cultivating a flower in a vase. He also explained that a flower arrangement could be placed in open air place at night (fig. 121).

Why did ancient scholars believe rainwater was favorable for use in both brewing tea and arranging flowers? In that agricultural era, there was no heavy industry, so the atmosphere was not polluted. Water from the sky was purer and cleaner than the water found in today's rainfall or snowfall (fig. 122). According to modern scientific analysis, the natural world only has rainwater and snowfall as sources of soft water, making it a good choice for creating the desired clear color and elegant aroma for brewing tea. When used to cultivate flowers, soft water also has excellent nourishing properties.

The concept of "harmony between heaven and man" is a common idea in traditional Chinese philosophy, forming a governing philosophy for human behavior. Taoist scholars said, "Humans are subject to the earth; the earth is subject to heaven; heaven is subject to the Tao; and Tao is subject to Nature." Confucians believed that "if one can praise the biological education given by heaven and earth, he can be united with heaven and earth." This so-called union with heaven and earth referred to humanity's proper place, subject to heaven, as being in accord with the laws and rhythms of the natural world. The essence of this way of thinking is rooted in an understanding of the eternal laws of the natural world, maintaining respect for the natural world, using natural resources in a rational manner, and realizing the dynamic, balanced development of man and nature in a symbiotic relationship.

Fig. 122 *Tea Gathering in Huishan* (detail)
Wen Zhengming
Ink and color on paper
Height 21.9 cm × Width 67 cm
Palace Museum, Beijing

This picture was painted in 1518, depicting Wen Zhengming and several poets in Huishan, Wuxi. One pair sits in the pit of a tea pavilion, while Wen Zhengming reads from a scroll and the other friends listen. Next to them, a boy prepares tea, boiling water from the well on the tea-brewing stove. There are various tea sets on the table.

CHAPTER 6
RELATED MATTERS

THE ORIGINAL TEXT

When a plum blossom has been arranged, the portion where the branch was broken off should be burned, then soaked in mud to make it more stable. When a peony has been arranged, the point where its branch was broken should be burned with the flame from a lamp and left until the smouldering stops on its own. When the campaka has been arranged, its roots should be crushed and rubbed in small amounts of salt. After a lotus has been arranged, the mass of its roots should be wound together and bound with hair, then mud should be used to seal the gaps. Once a crabapple has been arranged, its roots should be wrapped in tender mint leaves and put inside water. Aside from these particular cases, other flowers can be arbitrarily plucked and arranged, not being subjected to any inherent rules. The peony is most suitably stored with honey, which will keep it from rotting. Bamboo branches, hollyhock, garden balsam, and hibiscus should be put in hot water while being arranged, in order to keep the leaves from withering.

THE MODERN READER

The "related matters" addressed in this chapter are actually techniques used for preserving freshly cut flowers. When a flowering branch has first been arranged, appropriate measures should be taken to preserve the flower and prevent it from withering prematurely, thus extending the period during which it may be viewed. This section discusses various techniques used by the literati to extend the lifespan of flowering branches, including methods such as heat treatment, end-crushing, salt coating, and honey cultivation (fig. 123).

1. Ancient Methods of Flower Preservation

In ancient times, the following methods were often used to extend the lifespan of flowering branches:

Heat treatment. This included scalding portions of the branch or burning its end. The scalding method immersed the base of an herbaceous plant into hot water to protect it from bacterial infection and to block the catheter so that the sap could no longer flow out, which served to prolong the plant's flowering period. The burning method placed the end of the branch of ligneous flowers into a flame and scorched it, then cut some of the scorched parts, placed them in clear water, rinsed them, and put them into the vase.

End-crushing method. The end of some ligneous flowers' branches, such as magnolia, lilac, or gardenia, can be crushed to expand the water absorbing surface, prolonging the

life of the flower arrangement.

Salt-coating method. This method involved applying a little salt (or salt water) to an incision on the branch.

Honey cultivation method. Some cut flowers were dipped into honey water. This was effective for keeping flowers such as the peony or lotus fresh.

2. Methods for Preserving Plum Blossoms

The first flower Zhang Qiande mentions in his section on flower preservation is the plum blossom, stating that it should first be burnt at the broken portion, then sealed with mud.

Fig. 123 *Flowers on Four Screens*
Zhu Menglu (Qing Dynasty)
Ink on paper
Height 109 cm × Width 29 cm × 4
Zhu Menglu, a native of Jiaxing, Zhejiang Province, stands with Wang Li as representatives of the mainstream freehand flower-and-bird painting of Shanghai School.

In fact, preservation of plum blossoms is not limited to this method. Other Ming Dynasty records indicate the use of crucian carp soup or pork soup from which the oil was removed as a method for storing the branch. Preserving the plum blossom branches in this way prevented the water from freezing and made for generous flowering of the branches, with even the smallest stamens opening. However, the plum blossom is a noble flower, aromatic and elegant, so placing such water in the vase was greasy, sticky, and smelly, making it unadvisable. Since a flower arrangement was meant to be elegant, it was necessary to arrange it in a clean, elegant manner, so why would one resort to anything less in its preservation methods?

3. Methods for Preserving the Peony

The peony was highly respected during the Tang Dynasty, being honored as the national flower. Events for arranging the peony were held in the palace, with strict protocols in place regarding the flowers' appearance. There were strict regulations for where the flowers were to be placed, the cutting tools to be used, the quality of water to be provided, and the arrangements of lattices or paintings to be employed.

One can imagine how highly prized were the techniques for preserving the peony. The burning method was often used in arranging peonies. The branch was scorched with fire at the place where it had been cut to prevent the juices in the stem from flowing out, which would cause the flower to wither prematurely. This method also played a role in disinfection and sterilization.

Methods for arranging the peony were still evolving. In the Yuan Dynasty, Yu Zongben wrote in *Planting Tree Flowers* (*Zhong Shuhua*), "The herbaceous peony and peony are removed and burned, then placed in a vase with water. Its cut end is first sealed with wax." The Ming Dynasty text *The Illustrated Book on Agriculture* (*Bianmin Tuzuan*) by Kuang Fan describes in more detail that "the peony and herbaceous peony are placed into a vase after the branch is burned off, then sealed with wax. It is then immersed in water and left to soak for several days." These techniques are still in use today.

Modern floral arrangement includes the sucrose preservation method. Sucrose preservation is the treatment of cut flowers with high concentrations of sugar, which can increase the water absorption of cut flowers, preventing protein degradation and delaying the aging process of the flowers. This is similar to Zhang Qiande's method of honey cultivation for the peony.

4. Methods of Preserving the Lotus

After the lotus is picked, the flowering period is quite short, and the petals soon drop. It is necessary to carefully store the lotus in order to extend the period in which it may be viewed. Modern techniques for preserving cut lotus include the use of sucrose water to preserve freshness. Compared to clear water, sucrose water with an appropriate concentration can effectively improve the preservation period of the lotus.

5. Methods for Preserving Other Types of Flowers

For other flowers, including the gardenia, crabapple, bamboo branch, hollyhock, garden balsam, or hibiscus, the method of storing and preserving the cut flowers is less rigid. With its long flowering period, the gardenia can survive for a long time even if it is simply placed in clear water, making it a flower quite easy to care for. Crabapples should be covered with mint leaves, and in fact, its roots may even be burned. More delicate flowers such as hollyhock, garden balsam, and hibiscus are placed in a vase with boiled water to keep the leaves fresh.

There are other practical techniques for cutting flowers, such as shearing in water. This means the main stem is placed into a basin of water to prevent the air from infiltrating the stem tube and hindering the absorption of water. There is also a commonly used oblique cutting method, in which the branches are cut at an angle to increase water absorption.

CHAPTER 7
TABOOS

THE ORIGINAL TEXT

In general, there are six taboos in flower arrangement. The first is storing a flower in well water, and the second is failing to change the water over a long period of time. Third is manipulating the plant with oily hands. The fourth taboo is allowing cats or mice to destroy the plants, and the fifth is exposing it to smoke from incense, or burning coals after burning the oil lamp. The final taboo is hiding it away in a closed room and not exposing it to natural air. Anything that falls into one of the above categories is taboo in flower arranging.

THE MODERN READER

There are taboos in many fields of study, and flower arrangement is no exception. Here, Zhang Qiande cites six taboos in vase flower arrangement.

Well water should not be used in flower arrangements, as it does not allow flowers to flourish. It is preferable to use rainwater or river water. The water in the vase must be changed frequently. If it is not changed each day, it will grow turbid, and the flowers' colors will not be bright. If oily hands are used to manipulate the branches, they will be left sticky and no longer fresh. If a vase with flowers is placed in a closed room that is not ventilated or airy, the flowers will not receive air, light, or rain, turning them dull and timid, leaving them to wither easily. Exposure to too much smoke from incense will likewise harm the flowers. Cats and mice should also be prevented from damaging the plants. From this comment, we are reminded that cats were popular pets during the Ming Dynasty.

Among these six taboos, the most important thing to note is the proper placement of the vases. In ancient times, indoor illumination was achieved mainly by oil lamps or candles. Candles were expensive, and they burned quickly, so oil lamps were the most common method of indoor illumination. Oil for the lamps was mostly tung oil, emitting black smoke when the wick was ignited, which had an impact on the growth of flowering branches placed in vases. At the same time, the ash from the tung oil was black and its texture delicate. If the smoke from such a lamp reached a vase, the vessel was extremely difficult to clean. A good vase could easily be ruined by such smoke. However, there was also one almost magical effect: coal ash from these lamps could be used to trace the eyebrow. At that time, women were in the habit of collecting the ash from lamps to apply to the eyebrows as makeup. In addition, a famed ink was made by collecting the soot from burning tung oil.

CHAPTER 8
VASE MAINTENANCE

THE ORIGINAL TEXT

The only flowers to be found blooming in the winter are the narcissus, wintersweet, and plum blossom. During winter, it is appropriate to use ancient wares like *zun* and *lei* in flower arrangements. It is necessary to use a tin vessel inside the vase to hold water, which will avoid the danger of the vase cracking if the water freezes. If a porcelain vase is to be used, a small amount of sulfur must be placed into the water. The vase should be placed beneath a south-facing window during the day, to allow maximum proximity to sunlight. At night, it should be placed beside the bed, so that the flowers could absorb the human breath, and the water in the vase would not freeze. This is also achieved by removing a small layer of oil from pork soup, which is then placed in the water with the floral arrangement, keeping the vase from being damaged and allowing the flowers to bloom fully. Some flowers may be placed in a vase with hot boiled water. These should be placed in an ordinary vase with boiled water, and the vase's mouth must then be closed up tightly. After the water is cooled, it must be replaced with rainwater in a precious vase. The vase must never be damaged. If a precious vase is used to hold boiling water from the beginning, the vessel will surely be damaged. This must be avoided.

THE MODERN READER

This section discusses ways of protecting vases in water.

From the Song Dynasty onward, there were many types of vases (fig. 126), but all of them were open-mouthed. Such vessels as the *yuhu* spring vase, the plum vase, and the globular vase could not be equipped with liners, so Zhang Qiande suggested that it was appropriate to arrange flowers with open statues and wares, such as *zun* or *lei*, during the winter instead (figs. 124–125).

When using a small porcelain vase, it is possible to add sulfur to the water to prevent freezing. However, the anti-freezing effect of

Fig. 124   Dragon and Tiger Bronze Wine Vessel (*Zun*)

Shang Dynasty (1600–1046 BC)

Fig. 125   Ancient Urn-Shaped Bronze Wine Vessel (*Lei*)

Warring States Period (475–221 BC)

sulfur is not particularly good, so it is necessary to proceed with caution. For instance, when sulfur is used, the vase should be placed in a warm, sunny spot. At night, it should be placed next to the bed, close to human warmth, so that the water will not freeze.

Vase flower arrangements should be placed under a south-facing window in winter. This was not only to protect it from frost, but also to conform to the norms of Ming Dynasty gardening, a very developed field. Literati such as Zhang Qiande, who were born in wealthy homes, had a good deal of experience living in gardens. Regardless of its practical functions, garden architecture always paid close attention to creating a leisurely atmosphere. The natural landscape seen through a window should be unique, so a vase of flowers placed leisurely beneath a south-facing window was in line with the norms of gardening culture during the Ming Dynasty.

Fig. 126 *Decoration for Appreciation on the First Day of the Lunar Calendar*

Lu Hui (Qing Dynasty)
Ink and color on paper
Height 95 cm × Width 43 cm

This painting is in the typical late Qing Dynasty style. There are a wide range of artefacts in the painting, deliberately placed to create an atmosphere of wealth. The flowers include red plum blossoms in different vases, *lingzhi*, and calamus, alongside rockeries, ancient pots, fruits, and vegetables in a rich scene of the New Year.

HISTORY OF VASES
By Yuan Hongdao (Ming Dynasty)

INTRODUCTION

THE ORIGINAL TEXT

Because they have abandoned carnal entertainment, the world's hermits and sophisticates develop a great love of landscapes, flowers, and bamboo (fig. 128). These things have nothing to do with fame and fortune, and they will not be found by those seeking after worldly pursuits. Worldly people often live in places where there is great wealth and an accumulation of financial gains. Their eyes never tire of the things of the world, and their minds never grow weary of calculations. Even if they were to take possession of landscapes, flowers, and bamboos, they would have no time to care for them. For this reason, hermits can take temporary ownership of these things. Reclusive, elegant folk are actually in a realm without conflicts. Those who give up all to the world, even if they want to give the landscapes, flowers, and bamboo to others, others may not be willing to accept them. So, the reclusive folk are actually at ease and

On pages 94 and 95

Fig. 127 *Landscape and Figures II* (detail)
Please refer to page 117.

Fig. 128 *Landscape and Figure* (detail)
Chen Hongshou
Ink and color on paper
Height 33.4 cm × Width 27.3 cm
Freer Gallery of Art, Washington D.C.

In this painting, a nobleman sits in a mountain scene, holding a cup of wine and staring at the pine tress overhead and the blue sky beyond, completely at his ease. Behind the nobleman is a white glazed porcelain vase, as if waiting for the master to pluck flowers to fill it.

happily living among the landscapes, and will not get into any trouble when they menopolize this beauty.

Ah! But this is the life of a noble hermit. Being just a sober official, I cannot achieve such a life myself. Fortunately, though, I am now between retiring and resigning, and the things once so worth fighting for can no longer reach me. I just want to put on my hat and stand next on the banks of the rising rocks, washing my hat in its clear water (meaning to retire from worldly affairs). But shackled by a humble official position, I can only enjoy myself by planting many flowers and bamboos. The places where I have lived are often low-lying and small, and I have moved often. I have had to use small vases to arrange flowers, since they could be placed anywhere any time. The famous flowers planted by great people in the capital have become items placed upon my desk. There is no pruning of tress or flowers, but there is an appreciation of good taste. I have only taken a few flowers—I am not greedy. It has indeed been worthwhile to describe that others noted I had a hobby of appreciating flowers but none would compete with me. Ah! Arranging flowers in a vase is but a temporary pleasure, and it can never make you forget the real joy of natural scenery. For this reason, I intentionally make a record. All items concerning the arrangement of flowers in vases are described in turn and shared with those who, though not wealthy, love such things.

In the preface to *History of Vases*, Yuan Hongdao first mentions his hobby of landscaping and raising flowers and bamboo, emphasizing that such a hobby neither competes for any sort of profit in the world nor brings about any harm. These may be words written after Yuan's turbulent experiences in officialdom. Such an exclamation is quite different from Zhang Qiande's words in the preface to *On Vase Flower Arrangements*, from which we can see that he has a very different perspective on floral arrangements.

Zhang Qiande always had protection because of his family's position. He turned his back on worldly pleasures, but was a great collector of renowned paintings and calligraphies, only arranging flowers on occasion during his leisure time, and seldom considering what sorts of things might lead to trouble. By contrast, Yuan Hongdao served as an official in various parts of the country. His social experience was quite rich, and he basically had no hobbies of collecting renowned works. He felt that picking a few flowers and putting them on a table would bring no embarrassment to him. From this we see the complete difference between one who wandered widely and lived a more reclusive and poor life and one who was a wealthy idler embedded in his family's residential compound. Yuan Hongdao was only 43 years old at the time of his death. After he died, even the cost of his coffin and the travel costs for his family dependents to return to their hometown were borne by his friends, and his paintings, calligraphies and ink stones were also sold to make ends meet.

Fig. 129 *Offering Lotus* (detail)
Jiang Tingxi
Ink and color on silk
Height 141 cm × Width 62 cm
A single piece of lotus is usually arranged in a vase.

As he himself writes, Yuan was a person who did not like pursuing a political career, and wished to rid himself of worldly evils. He was a Buddhist, and he was often in contact with sophisticated monks. In fact, he studied Buddhism at a very deep level, and even wrote *Western Collaborative Theory* (*Xifang Helun*), one of the most significant Ming Dynasty writings of the Pure Land Sect (fig. 129).

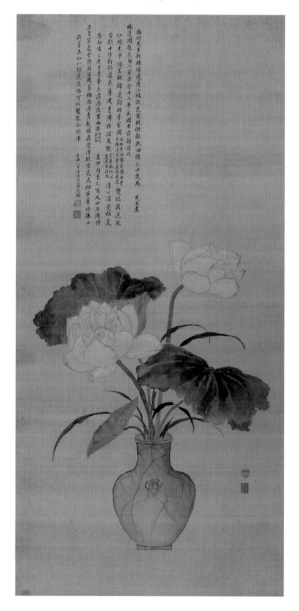

CHAPTER 1
CATEGORIES OF FLOWERS

THE ORIGINAL TEXT

Because Beijing's climate is so cold, most of the precious trees and flowers from the south cannot be found there, and even those that can be found are owned by powerful officials, eunuchs, and members of the imperial family. Generally, poor scholars are not able to enter the residents of these elite members of society, and so must seek out flowers in other nearby locales instead. Choosing flowers is like making friends. The noble men and women who live in the mountains or forests in seclusion are surrounded only by wild creatures, hiding themselves among the natural wilderness, so even if I wanted to make friends with them, it would be nearly impossible to do so. For this reason, I should set about making friends with those who live in developed urban areas and are considered talented people there, since these are the people in closer proximity to me, whom I can more easily get close to.

Likewise, in choosing flowers, I select those species that are most readily available, such as the plum blossom and crabapple in spring, the peony (fig. 130), herbaceous peony, and pomegranate flower in summer, the fragrant osmanthus, lotus, and chrysanthemum in autumn, and the wintersweet in winter. Within a single room, the flowers change with the seasons, with fragrance like that of Xun Yu, or beauty like the handsome He Yan, visiting my room like welcome guests. Although the flowers are taken from nearby this place, I always shy away from arbitrarily choosing mediocre flowers. Even though a branch of bamboo or cypress lacks flowers, I always opt to place it in a vase in favor of a flower of inferior quality. The *Book of Songs* says, "Even if there are no wise men who have experience and training in the world, there are always rules that can be followed." How can a mediocre person be integrated into the society of virtuous gentlemen? Such a thought is as laughable as that of taking a Huangfu family member as a recluse.

Fig. 130 *Peonies* (detail)
Yun Shouping
Ink and color on silk
Height 41 cm × Width 38.8 cm
Palace Museum, Taibei

This painting has two peonies depicted in the brushwork style in which Yun Shouping was skilled, with the pink and purple colors each enhancing the other's beauty.

In choosing flowers and flower materials, it is best to select seasonal flowers, which are elegant, beautiful, and worthy of admiration (fig. 131 and see fig. 133 on pages 102 and 103). If there is a lack of flowers at a particular period, it is preferable to place a few branches of bamboo or cypress into a vase instead. In this way, a poor scholar also has his own way of entertaining himself, since a small vase of flowers is enough to fill a room with its brilliance.

1. Standards for Selecting Plants and Flowers

During the Ming Dynasty, the art of vase flower arrangement was regarded as an activity for the gentrified class, particularly because it often required certain conditions. First, it needed a residential compound that bloomed with exotic flowers, gardens, and precious

Fig. 131 *Floral Scrolls* (detail)
Chen Chun
Ink on paper
Height 34.3 cm × Width 527.4 cm
Shanghai Museum

This scroll is painted in freehand style. It depicts dozens of flowers, including the orchid, chrysanthemum, lotus, sunflower, bamboo, and narcissus.

plants, all of which were carefully cultivated. The pursuit of exotic flowers and plants was common among wealthy families in the Ming and Qing dynasties. For instance, in *Treatise on Superfluous Things*, "Flowers and Trees" section, Wen Zhenheng commented on nearly every type of flower, stating which types were best, which valuable, and which inferior. For instance, among camellias, those from Yunnan and Sichuan were precious. Color mattered as well, with red more common, while yellow and white were more highly valued.

Yuan Hongdao lived as an official in Beijing, but did not spend his days living an extravagant life, nestled in a house with a courtyard or a scrumptious garden compound. The famed flowers brought from Jiangnan to the capital were not generally accessible to the poor. Yuan saw cultivating flowers as an activity similar to making friends. He did not expect to meet strangers who lived secluded in the mountains, so he found some aristocrats in the city with whom he could make friends, which was a good thing. For this reason, he was reluctant to set different standards for his selection of flowers and plants, so did not deliberately pursue exotic flowers. He understood appropriate compromise and concessions, and so sought

satisfaction and comfort within the limits of what he could afford. He collected flowers from the gardens of others' homes, so that even in his simple residence, there were plants and flowers he could admire. He was not choosy about his plants and flowers, but chose from those available nearby and placed them on his desk.

2. Frequent Choice of Seasonal Flowers

In this section, Yuan mentioned nine seasonal flowers he often used in vase arrangements: the plum blossom, crabapple, peony, herbaceous peony, pomegranate flower, osmanthus, lotus, chrysanthemum, and wintersweet. These seasonal flowers and plants were widely recognized, and were easily used in floral arrangements (see fig. 132 on page 102).

In the absence of flowers to pick, Yuan preferred to use bamboo or cypress branches. Bamboo was slender and upright, symbolic of the character of a gentleman. Placing bamboo in a vase was not only an elegant style, but also an extension of the spirit and culture of seclusion (see fig. 9 on page 14).

3. Culture Background

In this passage, several cultural elements are mentioned.

Ming Dynasty Eunuchs
During the Ming Dynasty, the group of eunuchs was one of the most formidable in Chinese history. Judging from official accounts and essays from the Ming Dynasty essayist Gui Youguang (1507–1571), the great eunuchs began to take power from the time of the Zhengde reign (1506–1521). In the late Ming Dynasty, the eunuch Wei Zhongxian (1568–1627) was so powerful he was almost like an emperor himself, skillfully manipulating the emperor. Yuan commented that the famous flowers of Jiangnan were not readily viewed by the general public, so where did they go? Yuan's first instinct is to assume they were at the residence of the imperial eunuch. He was frustrated by the thought of being prevented from seeing the various precious flowers he loved, since they were planted at the eunuchs'.

Xun Yu and He Yan
Xun Yu (163–212) was a mastermind of Cao Cao's (155–220) administration during the Eastern Han Dynasty, a man of great learning and high position. It is said that he was a great man and very attractive, full of grace and dignity, and with a pleasing aroma about him, known as "fragrance of Linggong" or "fragrance of Xunling." The important historical documents studying the ancient people and culture of Xiangyang, the *Record*

Fig. 132 *Decoration for Appreciation on Four Screens*
Li Yu (Qing Dynasty)
Ink and color on paper
Height 111 cm × Width 27 cm × 4

The four screens depict the chrysanthemum, peony, lotus, and orchid, which represent the four seasons. Though it inevitably falls into a stereotype, it is quite exquisite.

Fig. 133 *Floral Scrolls* (detail)

of Xiangyang (*Xiangyang Ji*) says that when he sat in someone else's home, his aroma lingered for three days. He left behind a classical allusion, "Xunling with lingering fragrance," which, like the term "Pan with fruits offered," became another moniker

to describe handsome men.

He Yan (d. 249) was the grandson of General He Jin (d. 189) of the Eastern Han Dynasty. His father died young, and his mother was taken as a concubine by Cao Cao. When he was still young, he was already very outstanding. Later he married Cao Cao's daughter, the princess, Jin Xiang. He Yan was a relative of the emperor, and was both attractive and well dressed. His face was delicate, fair and of unrivaled beauty. Sima Guang (1019–1086) reported that he was extremely vain, loving to dress up and always keeping his face well powdered. Even when he walked, he paid great attention to his bearing. Later generations took the phrase "He with face powdered" as an allusion to a man's pale, beautiful face.

Yuan Hongdao's metaphor for plants and flowers illustrated that, though they were not rare or exceptional, they were good, aromatic, and elegant.

Huangfu Family Poses as Hermit

The earliest hermits can be traced back to ancient times, but by the end of the Han Dynasty, the hermit's role had been clearly defined. Generally, a hermit was anyone who did not cooperate with the court, but still continued to have a certain level of cultural influence. Gradually, though, after the Wei and Jin dynasties, there was a tendency toward extreme seclusion and worldliness, which came to be the connotation of the term "hermit." Some hermits used their seclusion for utilitarian purposes, as a means of gaining honor. Some people in positions of authority similarly went to meet scholars in secluded mountains or forests in order to obtain the reputation of a patron.

The historical text *Book of Jin* (*Jin Shu*) records that in the second year of Long'an (399), Huan Xuan (369–404), the son of the influential minister of the Eastern Jin Dynasty and the politician Huan Wen (312–373), launched a rebellion and took control of the Eastern Jin Dynasty. Since the Wei and Jin dynasties, there have been hermits scattered throughout the pages of history, but during that period, there were none at all, so Huan Xuan felt he had lost face. In order to obtain a reputation as a patron, he promptly dispatched someone to find Huangfu Xizhi, the sixth generation grandson of Huangfu Mi (215–282). He first instructed the former to hide in the mountains, paying for various expenses from his own pocket, then made an imperial request of the former as a court writer. At the same time, he instructed Huangfu Xizhi to deliberately refuse, and then issued an edict to crown the latter as "a nobleman." This tale was passed down to generations, and was jokingly referred to as "posing as a hermit."

CHAPTER 2
GRADES

THE ORIGINAL TEXT

Of the three thousand beauties of the late Emperor Hancheng, Zhao Feiyan was ranked first. Madam Xing and Madam Yin were both doted by the Emperor Wu of Han. When Madam Yin saw the face of Madam Xing from a distance, she wept and sighed. From this, we see that beautiful women cannot help but envy beauty in others, even though they themselves are beautiful, as rare things must surpass all others in their category. If one requires a beautiful woman to ride in a vehicle with other equally beautiful women, letting virtuous talent and ordinary people racing together shoulder to shoulder, whose fault is this? Similarly, the plum blossom has several varieties, with the Multi-Petalled Plum, Green Plum, Jade Butterfly and Hundred-Leaf Plum being the top grades. The top grade of the crabapple is the *Xifu Zimian*. The highest grades of peony are of the *Huanglouzi*, Green Butterfly, Watermelon Pulp, Red, and Dancing Black Lion varieties. The top grade of herbaceous peony include Champion, Imperial Yellow Robe, and *Baozhuangcheng*. The pomegranate flower is represented by the highest grade Crimson, and *Zhongtai*. The top grades of lotus are *Bitai*, and *Jinbian*, while the highest grades of osmanthus are *Qiuzi*, and *Zaohuang*. The top grades of chrysanthemum are Crane Feather, *Xishi*, and *Jianrong*, while the top grade of wintersweet flower is the *Qingkouxiang*.

All of these flowers and plants are rare species. Poor scholars cannot possibly collect all of these at home, so I have only recorded these few simply as a way to evaluate the quality of various types, not to mix the ordinary beauty with the rarest beauties. The ancients said that if one obtained a word of praise which lived on in history, this glory surpasses the ceremonial robes bestowed by the nobility. Today, I am like a historian in the land of flowers, like Dong Hu, carefully recording the history of the garden, equivalent to the status of *The Spring and Autumn Annals (Chunqiu)*. How can I not be strict and prudent? Confucius says that the evaluation principles in the annals of every country have been privately applied to the *Spring and Autumn* annals. I am doing the same for the biography of flowers.

THE MODERN READER

The ranking of flowers has always been a tedious task. In his ranking, Yuan Hongdao began with a story from the Han Dynasty court, in an attempt to make it more interesting. He believed that ranking flowers and plants should not be merely a vulgar listing of these rankings, but should be seen as a sort of beauty contest in the land of flowers, comparable to the beauty contests by which the imperial harem was filled. These rare species of flowers and plants should be treated with a degree of respect and should not be confused with the rarer colors of each type of flower or plant (fig. 134–137).

Figs. 134–137 *Eight Flower Scroll* (detail)
Qian Xuan
Ink and color on paper
Height 29.4 cm ×
Width 333.9 cm
Palace Museum, Beijing

This scroll depicts eight types of flowers, including the crabapple, pear, apricot, narcissus, peach, and peony. Each flower is relatively independent, but when combined, they form a single composition. Its colors are elegant, and shading remarkable.

1. Grades of Flowers

Yuan Hongdao cites some famous types of flowers that were held in esteem during that time. It should be noted that his understanding of flowers and plants was as a source of pleasure, and not as a profession.

Plum Blossom
Multi-Petalled Plum: abundant flowers, leaves several layers thick, a bloom like a white lotus, an exceptional plum.

Green Plum (Prunus mume var. viridicalyx): butterfly shaped, single to semi-double bloom, white with green calyx (fig. 138).

Jade Butterfly: branch of pure-bred plum, double petals, white flower, buds purple or light red at the point, flowers turn white when full (fig. 139).

Hundred-Leaf Plum: a branch of pure-bred plum, with more than 20 petals, yellowish heart, small flower and densely packed.

Crabapple
Xifu Zimian (Purple Cotton in xifu): a species of kaido crabapple known for its bright color and numerous petals.

Peony
Huanglouzi (Yellow Building): a type of yellow peony, which some researchers have identified as *Yaohuang* (fig. 140)

Green Butterfly: green peony, of the "pea green" type, one of four famous peonies, a spherical flower, green when it opens, yellow-green or yellow-white when in full bloom, thick petals, does not bloom easily, drooping bloom, flowers late (fig. 142).

Watermelon Pulp: red peony, pink and double petals, large flower.

Red: bright red peony, with a variety of colors ranging from rose, red-purple, and pink, double bloom, large flowers.

Dancing Black Lion (purple): according to the book *Flower Mirror* (*Hua Jing*) by horticulturalist Chen Haozi in the Qing Dynasty, a variety of the pink peony, many leaves, five purple petals at core.

Herbaceous Peony (fig. 141)
Champion: red varieties of the herbaceous peony, according to Song Dynasty official and poet Wang Guan's *Book of Yangzhou Herbaceous Peony* (*Yangzhou Shaoyao Pu*) "has a crown of dark red with four or five circles around the top, in dense clusters. It is half a *chi* wide (roughly 15 cm) and six *cun* tall (roughly 18 cm), and brightly colored. Its beauty and fragrance surpasses others, thus giving it its name. The branches are hard and the leave sparse."

Imperial Yellow Robe: yellow varieties of the herbaceous peony. The *Book of Yangzhou Herbaceous Peony* records, "The Imperial Yellow Robe is a light yellow with sparse leaves, a slightly deep stamen scattered among leaves, which also have traces of green. It is an unrivaled flower."

Baozhuangcheng (Great Makeup): a purple

Fig. 138   **Green Plum**

Fig. 139   **Jade Butterfly Plum**

Fig. 140 *Yaohuang* Peony

Fig. 142 Paeonia Suffruticosa "Pea Green" (Peony)

variety of herbaceous peony, described in *Books of Various Flowers* as "light purple, with at least twelve large leaves, which cling closely around the flower. It is eight to nine *cun* tall (roughly 24 to 27 cm) and half a *chi* wide (roughly 15 cm). On each small leaf, there are gold veins decorated with jade beads. It is as fragrant as an orchid, a rare flower. Its branches are hard and flat. The queen of the purple variety."

Fig. 141 *Herbaceous Peonies*
Yun Shouping
Ink and color on silk
Height 226.6 cm × Width 74.8 cm
The Cleveland Museum of Art, Cleveland

Yun Shouping was renowned for his flower paintings in the early Qing Dynasty. His work focuses on the styling of objects, with the flavor of the literati. This piece was completed in 1685. Its composition is simple, including a cluster of herbaceous peonies on both left and right, depicted in rich red, white, pink, and purple tones, with green leaves drawing the whole together. The painting is very detailed, and its color set elegant. Yun Shouping here demonstrates his typical style of floral paintings.

Fig. 143 *Double Lotus*

Giuseppe Castiglione
Ink and color on silk
Height 109.3 cm ×
Width 58.7 cm

In this painting, alongside the twin lotus flower and lotus seedpods, there are also two heavy ears of grain. This is not by chance, but is a response to the tastes of emperors Yongzheng (1678–1735) and Kangxi, who both liked agricultural scenes. The flowers in the vase suggest a bumper crop of harvest, an auspicious sign, presumably meant to further please the emperors.

Pomegranate Flower (fig. 144)

Crimson, and *Zhongtai* (Terrace): a deep red pomegranate with layers of petals, primarily for appreciation.

Lotus

Bitai (Green Terrace) and *Jinbian* (Colored Border) : referring to two types of double-colored lotus with layers of petals (fig. 143), the *Book of Various Flowers* records that "close to the Southern capital, at Li Honglu's residence (*Translator's note*: Honglu is an official title), a species was obtained, called *Jinbian* with a green base and white petal. The green bud contains a line of red. When opened, each leaf is similarly dyed red on the edges. It is a very unusual species, and I planted it together with *Bitai* in two separate ponds made with bricks, or in the big container, for appreciation on the table."

Osmanthus

Qiuzi (Ball) and *Zaohuang* (Early Yellow): rare species of the fragrant osmanthus, *Qiuzi* refers to a dense flower, while *Zaohaung* refers to one that flowers early; in the literary monograph of the Ming Dynasty writer Wang Shimao entitled *On Horticulture and Gardening: Flowers* (*Xuepu Zashu and Huashu*), we read, "The *Zaohuang* opens in mid-July, and the fragrance of the *Qiuzi* is the best, filling the grounds."

Chrysanthemum

Crane Feather: referring to the various colors of this type; *Book of Various Flowers* records, "Yellow Crane Feather have petals like gold, with red along the back of the petal. When it opens, it is a stunning effect of yellow haloed by red. The leaves are green, the stem thin and with numerous thorns. Its branches are purple-black. It is strong as steel and can grow as high as seven or eight *chi* (roughly 210 to 240 cm), and it is a fairy among chrysanthemums. The light-yellow Crane Feather is rarely seen, followed by white, then

Fig. 144 *Flowers and Plants*

Zhang Xin (Qing Dynasty)

This painting depicts a very unique flowering branch with three kinds of flowers, magnolia, pomegranate, and iris. The magnolia flowers are from early to mid-March, the iris from April to June, and the pomegranate in May. Sadly, the only way to see these flowers in bloom at the same time is in a painting.

In traditional floral-themed paintings, the iris rarely makes an appearance, and it is particularly unusual that it would be drawn with the magnolia and pomegranate. Usually, the magnolia is painted alongside the crabapple, and pomegranate appear alongside the calami. In this painting, the lavender iris is matched with the red pomegranate, which is truly innovative.

pink, then purple."

Xishi (Beauty): divided into categories such as Golden *Xishi*, White *Xishi*, Light-Yellow *Xishi*, *Yuban* (Jade Plate) *Xishi* and Silver Red *Xishi*.

Jianrong (literally "cutting the fur"): Yellow *Jianrong*, White *Jianrong* and Purple *Jianrong*. The petals are short and broad, with splitted ends (fig. 145).

Wintersweet

Qingkouxiang: or chimonanthus praecox var. grandiflorus, a round-petalled, yellow flower with a purple center and a strong fragrance.

2. Cultural Background

Several cultural items are mentioned in this passage.

Yin and Xing Avoid Meeting

Fighting was fierce in the Han court. The Emperor Wu of Han (156–87 BC) favored both Madam Yin and Madam Xing. In order to avoid a quarrel between them, it was a matter of policy that the two never be allowed to meet. Madam Yin asked the

emperor to let her see Madam Xing and, after considering it, he agreed. He first introduced an imposter, but after seeing her, Madam Yin said, "Her bearing is not that of Madam Xing." So Madam Xing put on old clothing and came alone. Seeing her from afar, Madam Yin said, "Ah, this is real!" Then, lowering her head, she wept and sighed, wishing she were more like Madam Xing. From then on, the two women avoided each other.

Dong Hu and the *Spring and Autumn Annals*

The highest standard for Chinese historians is to write in a straightforward way and tell the truth, rather than allowing those in power to manipulate it. The ancient Chinese history and literary classic *Commentary of Zuo* (*Zuo Zhuan*) records that when the Jin Kingdom

Fig. 145 *Painting Expressing Tao Yuanming's Poetry* (detail)
Shi Tao (1642–1708)
Ink and color on paper
Height 27 cm × Width 21.3 cm
Palace Museum, Beijing

Tao Yuanming often used chrysanthemums to represent himself, with the flower's resilient nature expressing his own lofty moral integrity and feelings. In this painting, chrysanthemums are blooming within a fenced yard, and a recluse is holding up a chrysanthemum and admiring it, his manner leisurely. The painter admired Tao's noble sentiment, and was also using the character and flowers in the painting to express his own thoughts and feelings.

Fig. 146 *Dialogue*
Chen Hongshou

This painting depicts seated figures discussing philosophy. The literati, who is speaking, sits at a small stone table, which holds a vase containing a small autumn leaf clipping. From this, we see that scholars thought it necessary to have vases of flowers to serve as props when they lectured.

emperor Jin Linggong was in power (620–607 BC), he lost his sense of morality and did great harm to the people. On numerous occasions, Zhao Dun, the ruling minister, painstakingly counseled the emperor, but to no avail. In fact, people were sent to assassinate Zhao Dun, forcing him to flee to the hinterlands of Jin territory. Upon hearing that Linggong had been killed by his brother Zhao Chuan, he returned to the capital and continued to govern. At that time, the official historian Dong Hu recorded the incident, calling it "Zhao Dun Killing the King," and declared it to the courtiers to make the record clear. Zhao Dun argued that it was not his crime. Dong Hu said, "As ruling minister, since you did not cross the national border, the righteousness of the monarchy was not cut off. When you returned, you should have organized men to fight for what is right. If you do not, you should be accused of murdering the monarch." Confucius praised Dong Hu, calling him "a good historian of ancient times."

Confucius had high praise for this sort of writing. When he compiled *The Spring and Autumn Annals*, he followed Dong Hu's method. It implicitly includes both praise and criticism in its narrative, expressing the writer's subjective value judgements in euphemistic terms, known as "the Spring-and-Autumn style" (fig. 146).

Yuan Hongdao mentions these to show that he is very cautious when writing about trees and plants. At the same time, he tells the reader that his like and dislike of various flowers are merely a matter of preference, and are clearly subjective judgements.

CHAPTER 3
VESSELS

THE ORIGINAL TEXT

Like the flowers themselves, the vessels used for vase flower arrangements are delicate. Just as courtiers such as Concubine Yang and Zhao Feiyan could not be housed in shabby thatched cottages, or as wine connoisseurs like Ji Kang, Ruan Ji, He Zhizhang, and Li Bai could not be entertained in small roadside eateries, so an arrangement of fine flowers deserves appropriately elegant accommodations. In Jiangnan, I have seen an ancient bronze *gu* used to hold a flower arrangement. Its color was green, and it was seamless, with small specks of sand on the outside. Used as a vase, it was called a golden house for the flowers. Further, kiln ware such as that from the Guan Kiln, Ge Kiln, Xiang Kiln, and Ding Kiln are meticulously crafted, and thus serve as suitable accommodations for a floral arrangement.

Generally, a vase that is to be placed in a room should be relatively short and elaborate. Bronzeware suited for the purpose includes flower *gu*, bronze *zhi*, *zun* and *lei*, square Han pots, plain pots, flat shaped pots, and so forth. Kiln ware includes paper mallet vases, gooseneck vases, eggplant bag vases, flower *zun*, flower sacks, small yarrow vases and cattail mallet vases. Those selected for vase flower arrangements should be short, so that they can sit easily on a desk. If the vase is too large, how is it any different from the vessels used to hold incense burned to the household's ancestors? Even if a large vase is an old artifact, it still looks tacky. Of course, there are various sizes of flowering branches, with flowers such as peony, herbaceous peony, and lotus being relatively large. Naturally, there is no limit on the size of vases for such plants and flowers, and large vases can be used to display them.

I have heard that if it has been buried in the earth for a long time, ancient bronzeware absorbs an earthy quality. When used to store flowers, the blooms tend to be exceptionally bright, opening quickly and taking longer to wither, and even bear fruit after they do wither. Ancient pottery has a similar effect. From this, we see that old, precious vessels are not only delightful in themselves, but also serve to intensify the effects of the flowers they hold. However, people born to poor families or of a lowly background may have one or two bottles from the Xuande or Chenghua period, and even that is enough to give them a reputation for having a bit of wealth.

In winter flower arrangements, a tin vessel should be used to line the vase. The northern climate is cold, and when water in a bronze—not to mention porcelain—vessel freezes, the vase will break. A little sulphur placed in the water will also prevent freezing.

THE MODERN READER

Arranging flowers was originally an activity limited to the upper class. Yuan Hongdao mentions that when he was traveling in Jiangnan, he once saw a rich household that used an antique bronze vessel for a flower arrangement, and it made an impression on him (fig. 147).

1. Bronzeware Suitable for Use in Flower Arrangements

Flower *gu*. There were three main parts of a Ming Dynasty flower *gu*: the bell-shaped mouth, a drum belly in the middle, and a phoenix tail shaped base. It was a simple, elegant device.

Bronze *zhi*. This was a vessel for drinking wine. Like *zun*, it was small, with a round belly, extravagant mouth, and ring foot. Most were with lids. They were popular as wine goblets from the Shang Dynasty until the Western Zhou Dynasty.

***Zun* and *lei*.** This refers to types of vessel for drinking wine.

Square Han pots. This was a square copper pot from the Han Dynasty. The Han pots inherited the traditional style of the Spring and Autumn Period and the Warring States Period. Round pots were called "bells" and square pots *fang*. These vessels were used to contain both wine and water. During the Han Dynasty, they were also used as measuring devices.

Fig. 147 *Decoration for Appreciation*
Sha Fu (Qing Dynasty)
Ink and color on paper
Height 125 cm × Width 31 cm
Sha Fu, a native of Suzhou, Jiangsu Province, was born to a family of artists. He excelled in painting figures, ladies, and flowers, and made his living as an artist. He was one of the city's most famous painters at the Lunar New Year paintings store in Shantang, outside Changmen gate in Suzhou.

Plain pot. This was a type pf non-textured bronze wine maker with a mouth shaped like a clove of garlic. It was especially suitable for displaying flowers like the peony and herbaceous peony, since it had the smallest mouth (fig. 148).

Flat shaped pot. This was a type of flat bronze pot.

2. Porcelain Suitable for Use in Floral Arrangements (fig. 149)

Many of the vases mentioned by Yuan Hongdao are similarly praised by Zhang Qiande. Here, we will introduce only those items that have not been introduced in previous chapters.

Flower *zun*. A type of porcelain flower pot with a large open mouth and small belly. Its name alludes to an imitation bronze wine vessel *zun*. Many such pots were made in Song Dynasty Ding Kiln.

Flower sack. A form of porcelain vase, usually with a flat belly and spherical body. It was very popular in the Ming and Qing dynasties.

Cattail mallet. This refers to a cattail mallet vase, which has straight mouth, short and straight neck and a long body. It was shaped like the ear of a cattail, giving its name.

3. Porcelain of the Xuande and Chenghua Years

Here, Yuan Hongdao laments, wondering how ordinary folk could come by such treasures. If one had one or two vases made during the Xuande and Chenghua year, he was considered a "pauper turning rich overnight." This phrase is not an exaggeration.

The porcelain produced in the official kilns during the Xuande and Chenghua reigns hold a very important position in the history of the development of Chinese porcelain. During the Xuande years, the blue-and-white

Fig. 148 *The Rich Vase*
Zhu Zhanji
Ink and color on paper
Height 110.5 cm × Width 54.4 cm
Palace Museum, Taibei

Zhu Zhanji, Emperor Xuanzong of Ming, loved to paint and write calligraphies. He was particularly keen on painting landscapes, figures, animals, bird and flower pieces, and insects. This painting by the royal pen was composed in 1429. It depicts a copper hanging vase, containing just three peony flowers. The center flower is green and hangs above the beam, very detailed and interesting. The peony is rich in implication, and beneath it is a cat (read in Chinese as *mao*), a homophone for the character *mao* (耄), which conveys wishes for longevity.

porcelain fired at the Jingdezhen Imperial Kiln reached a pinnacle, while the *doucai* porcelain from the Chenghua period had a thin, light body, smooth glaze, bright colors, and elegant patterns. In 2004, a Chenghua "*doucai* chicken cup" sold for HK$281 million at Sotheby's Spring Auction in Hong Kong. Even during the Ming and Qing dynasties, the porcelain from the Xuande and Chenghua kilns was rare and valuable.

4. Cultural Background

Several cultural items are mentioned in this passage.

Yang Yuhuan and Zhao Feiyan

During the Song Dynasty, it was generally believed that the Tang Dynasty fell from prosperity, despite its strength, due to Emperor Xuanzong's (685–762) doting on Concubine Yang, which ultimately led to the "An and Shi Chaos" and the fall of the empire, just as Zhao Feiyan (d. 1 BC) was spoiled by the Han emperor, leading to the demise of the Han Dynasty. These two peerless beauties are considered the root of the respective dynasties troubles.

From the beginning of the Northern Song Dynasty, the phrase "Yuhuan and Feiyan" came to be widely used among the literati to ridicule old ways. During the Ming and Qing dynasties, the phrase was mainly used in the

Fig. 149 *Decoration for Appreciation*
Zou Yigui (1686–1772) and Giuseppe Castiglione
Qing Dynasty
Ink and color on silk
Height 71 cm × Width 31 cm × 4

There are numerous Qing Dynasty paintings from the folk and the court depicting decorations for appreciation on the first day of the lunar calendar as Spring Festival-themed works. This four-screen work was collaboration between two artists. It depicts narcissus, fingered citron, wintersweet and nandina, all auspicious flowers pointing to the Spring Festival.

context of arranging flowers. Scholars used the term to describe the beauty of the peony and crabapple.

"Golden House" for Flowers

A tale from the Han court about, "living in a golden house to keep one's mistress" is not derived from history, but is derived from the bizarre novel *The Story of Hanwu* (*Hanwu Gushi*) which depicts the life of the Emperor Wu of Han.

When Princess Guantao saw the young Emperor Wu of Han, she pointed to her daughter, saying, "What do you think of Ah Jiao?" The emperor smiled and replied, "Well, if I can take Ah Jiao as my wife, I'll keep her in a golden house." Hearing this, Princess Guantao was so delighted and begged the Emperor Jing of Han (188–141 BC) to sanction a marriage. This story was passed down from the Han court and widely known by later generations.

CHAPTER 4
SELECTING WATER

THE ORIGINAL TEXT

The spring waters of Biyun Temple (Temple of Azure Clouds) on Xi Shan in the capital, of Liebo Lake, or of Longwangtang are all suitable for use in floral arrangements. Once the Gaoliang Bridge has been passed, the waters become contaminated and should not be used. It is best to place water in the vase only after exposing it to the breeze and sunlight. As for other water sources, such as that in the Mulberry Garden, Manjing, Shawo, or the Mother Wang Well (referring to ancient wells in the capital), though these waters are sweet, flowers will not grow if water from these sources is used for the arrangement. Bitter water is particularly taboo in flower arrangements, because such water is too salty. It is better to store extra water from the rainy season. This should be done according to the following method: when rainwater enters the grate, a piece of red-hot coal should be added. This will allow it to be stored for years without any deterioration in its quality. Such water is not only useful for nourishing flowers, but also for brewing tea.

THE MODERN READER

Because he loved to visit mountains and rivers, Yuan Hongdao had a nuanced understanding of the beauty of landscapes, and he demonstrates much better taste in landscapes than in artefacts. His best-known writings were travel notes. From this background, selecting water for use in floral arrangements was his specialty (fig. 150).

Yuan Hongdao traveled extensively in the west outskirts of Beijing, and he had broad experience with all the neighboring springs. The garden-style Biyun Temple was located on north side of Xiangshan Park. First built in 1331, it was continuously expanded through the Ming and Qing dynasties. There was a courtyard housing a natural spring on the north side of the temple, called "Spring Waters." The spring flowed out of a seam in the stones, from which it fell into a pool. It was sweet and refreshing. Liebo Lake was located on the eastern side of Yuquan Mountain in the northwestern outskirts of Beijing. Yuquan Mountain was famous for its spring water, which was of exceptional quality. During the Ming and Qing dynasties, these springs were the sources of water for the court's use, and were called "the world's best springs." Liebo Lake was still a public touring area in the Ming Dynasty, but by the Qing Dynasty, it was encircled by the Jingming Garden, an imperial garden, and ordinary travelers were no longer able to visit it. Longwangtang was located in a temple on Pingpo Mountain in Beijing's western parts, at the eight great

Fig. 150
Landscape and Figures II

Chen Hongshou
Ink and color on paper
Height 33.4 cm × Width 27.3 cm
Freer Gallery of Art, Washington D.C.

In this painting, a scholar sits in a small boat, afloat on the river. The boat is moored amid a scene of serenity. He holds a scroll, studying at leisure, and in the bow of the boat is a vase of flowers, facing the scroll. With this scholar even carrying a vase flower arrangement on the boat, the depth of his love for such items is clearly evident.

temples of Western Hills. It was famous for the Dragon Spring, whose waters flowed year-round and were always sweet.

The Gaoliang Bridge, was built in the Yuan Dynasty, the 29th year of Kublai Khan's reign (1292), a historical bridge in the western outskirts of Beijing. By the Ming and Qing dynasties, ancient temple compounds were located there. At the time, the emperor's ministers, men, women, and children sat in its shade on the banks during the summer. Located at the bridgehead were the wine houses and teahouses. Tourists would flock there daily, making their way to the areas outside the capital.

Yuan Hongdao took great pleasure in visiting mountains and waters. He utilized these experiences in his writing of the *History of Vases*, describing where to find water suitable for flower arrangements in the capital and its surrounds. In fact, prestigious families in Beijing could be quite particular about the water, and Yuan Hongdao might not make a special trip to a place to get spring water to grow flowers, but this did not prevent him from entering into a theoretical discussion concerning the best water for use in floral arrangements.

CHAPTER 5
PROPRIETY

THE ORIGINAL TEXT

Flower arrangements should be neither too dense nor too sparse. At most two or three varieties of flowers are placed in a vase, and their heights should be staggered and their density irregular, like the composition of an exquisite painting. One should avoid placing vases in pairs, and avoid dullness and a lack of variety. Linear arrangements and the use of strings to hold the flowers up are likewise to be avoided. The so-called ordinariness of the flower arrangement lies in the fact that the length of its branches is scattered and the composition of the overall image is derived from nature. It is natural like Su Shi's essays, and like Li Bai's poetry, not rigidly adhering to certain conventions, but instead arranged naturally, which is true tidiness and order. If the flowering branches are all trimmed to the same length and the flowers matched according to color, it is like a tree planted at the front door of a government office, or like the tablet that stands in front of a tomb. Is this orderliness, or merely timidity?

THE MODERN READER

Yuan Hongdao believed that flower arrangements should be composed so as to look natural, with varying heights and density, saying that was the correct approach to flower arranging. This is consistent with Yuan's literary pursuits (fig. 151).

1. Floral Art and Literary Art

Yuan Hongdao was a leader of the Ming Dynasty anti-revival literary movement. Before the Ming Dynasty, the Central Plains area of China had undergone a foreign invasion, resulting in a cultural divide. After the establishment of the Ming Dynasty, the intelligentsia could not wait to restore old cultural traditions. They had a strong tradition of respecting the ancient and seeking to revive it. Yuan Hongdao was opposed to this movement, believing that a text should be rooted in its own times. Why should it look backward? In response, he put forward the idea of "an independent, unique spirit, not bound by convention."

He introduced a similar "spirit" in his floral arrangements, bringing a deeper cultural connotation to floriculture.

2. Cultural Background

Su Shi, a leader in the Northern Song Dynasty literary scene, made outstanding contributions in prose, poetry, lyric essays, calligraphy, and

Fig. 151 *Drying Hair*
Chen Hongshou
Ink and color on paper
Height 105 cm × Width
58 cm
Chongqing China Three
Gorges Museum

Xifa or drying hair originally points to drying one's hair in the open air, but later also to washing it. In this painting, a nobleman with his hair hanging to his shoulders looks like he is drinking. It is both exaggeratedly grotesque and extremely candid. The vase depicted in the painting is a flat-bellied porcelain vessel, so white as to be almost transparent. It holds bamboos and chrysanthemums in a casual way, creating a uniquely unrestrained atmosphere in the piece.

painting. He was very broad-minded and straightforward, and was always surrounded by good friends, good food, and good taste, though he was also a frequent and skilled traveler to the mountains. Li Bai (701–762), a great poet of the Tang Dynasty, admired swordsmanship and bravery. He also liked to travel, and he toured extensively through both the north and the south.

Li Bai and Su Shi are two older literary figures idolized by Yuan Hongdao. The pair shared some characteristics. They were straightforward, broad-minded, and passionate, and they expressed their true, unique feelings toward life in their writing. Neither was hypocritical or pretentious, and they both loved traveling among the mountains and rivers of their motherland.

CHAPTER 6
ESCHEWING WORLDLINESS

THE ORIGINAL TEXT

When flower arrangements are placed in a room, they need nothing more than a natural table and a rattan bed. The table placed in the room should be broad and heavy, and constructed of smooth, delicate materials. All the furniture, including lacquer tables with sidebars, mother-of-pearl beds with decorative patterns traced with gold, painted lacquer vases and frames, which are locally produced, should not be used.

THE MODERN READER

In a room containing a flower arrangement, the indoor furnishings should be elegant and refined, and never grandiose or gauche.

The natural tables and rattan beds that are highly recommended in this article are extremely elegant pieces of furniture.

The natural tables were most likely used in halls or studies. Wen Zhenheng's *Treatise of Superfluous Things* records, the natural tables "could be made of a few natural woods such as rosewood, lignumvitae, phoebe zhennan, or other types of wood. A large, broad table is highly valued, of not more than eight *chi* (roughly 240 cm) long and not more than five *cun* (roughly 15 cm) thick. The flying eaves must not be too sharp, but must instead be round, according to the ancient style. If there is a tail under the Japanese-style table, it is even better, and it should not have four feet commonly seen on desks. It is preferable to use either the root of an old tree or a piece of wood. If the desk top is broad and thick, then leave the center empty, with carved clouds, or with a *ruyi* pattern. There should not be carvings of a dragon-and-phoenix motif or of plants and flowers."

The rattan bed is a day bed for the family to lounge on. With a rattan surface at its center, it is softer and more comfortable than a wooden bed. Because of its simple design, it could be used in the study for lounging while reading a book or enjoying the scenery. It was very pleasant (fig. 152).

The *luodian* or mother-of-pearl bed was a luxurious wooden one, which Yuan Hongdao thought quite gaudy. This craft embeds into the surfaces of objects thin slices made of spiral shells or ground seashells and shaped as figures, birds, geometric patterns. These magnificent pieces of furniture had a very strong visual effect.

Fig. 152 *Wang Yuanqi's Appreciation of Chrysanthemums* (detail)

Yu Zhiding (1647–1716)
Ink and color on silk
Height 32.4 cm × Width 136.4 cm
Palace Museum, Beijing

This painting depicts the painter and calligrapher Wang Yuanqi in a garden of chrysanthemums. Wang's demeanor is leisurely, communicating elegant grace. The vase flower arrangements on the stand, and the scrolls, calligraphies, and paintings on the couch, all reflecting Wang's pastimes, and his elegance.

Ming Dynasty Elegance and Popularity

There are two Ming Dynasty texts that offer a view of the different living conditions of various groups at that time. Representative of elegant culture was Wen Zhenheng's *Treatise on Superfluous Things*, while the long novel *The Plum in the Golden Vase* (*Jin Ping Mei*) is representative of popular culture, which is a depiction of a family's daily life.

The mountain dwelling described in the *Records of Leisure Items* is arranged so that "it is bright and clean, and not too spacious." The bright and clean look is refreshing, but too much space stresses the eye. Or, one may install a window-sill beside the eaves or a corridor leading into the room, all designed according to the terrain. Appropriately, the atrium should be bigger and planted with flowers and trees, and decorated with bonsai. In the summer the door and window facing north should be taken out, linking the front and the back of the house, and providing greater ventilation. Some rice water can be sprinkled in the courtyard so that after the

rain, thick, green, lovely moss will grow. Around the foundation of the house, green cloud grass may be planted so that at its most luxuriant state, it would be verdant and sway in the wind. The courtyard wall should not be too tall, and some bury the roots of climbing fig under the wall, watering it with fishy water, causing the plant to climb up the wall. Even though this creates a mysterious flavor, it is still not as good as a plain white wall."

In *The Plum in the Golden Vase*, Ximen Qing's study was arranged in this way: "Inside the study, there was cool gilded bed of marbled black lacquer, placed at ground level and surrounded with a curtain of green yarn. In the painted-lacquer, gold-outlined bookshelves were books, handkerchiefs, cloth, and stationeries for gifts. Under the green screen window was a black lacquer zither table, a single mother-of-pearl chair placed beneath it. In the bookcase were letters, invitation cards, and account books on gifts for the Mid-Autumn Festival."

CHAPTER 7

HINDRANCES TO FLOWER CULTIVATION

THE ORIGINAL TEXT

It is not appropriate to burn incense beneath a flower arrangement, just as it is not appropriate to put pieces of fruit into tea. Tea has its own flavor and does not require any added sweetness or bitterness. In the same way, flowers have their own fragrance and do not need added aromas from incense. Burning incense will only detract from the charm of the flowers and damage their aroma. This sort of fault is too often committed by the layman. Even more, the smell of incense is hot and intense. Once it attacks the flowers in the vase, the flowering branches will wither, so incense will damage the flower. Joss sticks and incense sticks are especially taboo, as they contain musk. In the past, Han Xizai used to say that it is appropriate to burn camphor while appreciating the osmanthus. It is suitable to use agarwood while appreciating rosa rubus. Orchids should be matched with "four treasures,"

the banana shrub should be matched with musk, and the champaka with sandalwood. Such practice is tantamount to adding meat to bamboo shoots—the style of a bureaucrat's court chef rather than that of the literati. As for burning candles and oil lamps in the room, these could all kill the flowers, and should be quickly removed. Wouldn't it be appropriate to call such practices "hindrances to flower cultivation?"

Figs. 153–154
Luohan

Anonymous (Qing Dynasty), presumably Song Xu
Ink and color on silk
Height 28.6 cm × Width 29.2 cm
The Metropolitan Museum of Art, New York

In the painting on the left, a monk recites scriptures in the mountains. Two wild roses plucked from the mountains have been inserted into small blue glazed vases. Beneath the vase, incense burns in a small incense burner. In the painting on page 122, a venerable monk is meditating on a rock, and a boy holds a vase of flowers, supporting the monk. The celadon vase in the boy's hand holds white wild flowers.

THE MODERN READER

Burning incense alongside flowers was the usual practice of many noblemen of the Tang and Song dynasties. Not burning incense and simply taking in the natural fragrance of the flowers, so that the interior of a room was elegant and pleasant, was a practice more worthy of imitation. According to many members of the nobility who loved incense, their offering flowers would not conflict with burning incense. In such cases, incense might be lit alongside a floral arrangement.

1. Incense

Before the Sui and Tang dynasties, many higher quality types of incense were used for trade with the hinterland and other countries. The quantities of such incense that was available was quite small, so they were mainly used by the aristocracy and royal family. From the Tang Dynasty on, the literati, pharmacists, physicians, and Buddhist and Taoist monks engaged in incense-making. Special studies were made of the origin, properties, processing, functions, and compatibility of various spices, popularizing "incense culture" among scholars.

Joss sticks. The core of these incense sticks were made with slim sticks of bamboo or other fine woods as their core. They were relatively cheap and easy to use.

Blended sticks (*Hexiang*). The aromas of these sticks were made from a variety of complex expensive ingredients.

Camphor. Also known as "borneol," this fragrance is obtained through the steam distillation and recrystalization of blumea balsamifera (or borneol) stems and leaves. It was used for traditional incense and as an aromatic remedy in traditional Chinese medicine.

Agarwood. This fragrance is made from the resin secreted from agarwood. It sinks in water, so it is called sinking incense.

Four Treasures. This refer to four combined fragrances. The Ming Dynasty writer Zhou Jiazhou recalls, "Blended Four: one *liang* (roughly 37 g) of agarwood and sandalwood respectively, and one *qian* (roughly 3 g) of camphor and musk, burning as usual."

Sandalwood. Sandalwood has a calm, elegant aroma, and it can have a calming effect on the mind. It is mostly used when praying to Buddha.

Ancient people believed that incense and medicine were of the same origin, so the production of traditional incense was achieved through processes very similar to traditional Chinese medicine and Taoist alchemy. It required selection and concoction of the incense, deployment of the fragrant herb, determining compatibility, blending, producing, and storing. This elaborate process involved countless mechanisms at each step. The borneol, agarwood, musk, and sandalwood mentioned here are among the best traditional incense. Their production process was complex and expensive, making them beyond the reach of ordinary citizens.

2. Cultural Background

Several cultural items are mentioned in this passage.

Han Xizai (902–970)

He was a Southern Tang official during the Five Dynasties, a good writer, works including *On Proposal* (*Niyi Ji*) and *On Residence* (*Dingju Ji*), which are no longer extant. Han Xizai was known for his warm reception of female entertainers and hangers-on at home, which attracted many guests. The Southern Tang painter Gu Hongzhong painted *Han Xizai's Banquet Night*, depicting scenes of Han holding banquets at home.

The Way of Incense

This was a part of the elegant culture of the nobility. Both incense and vase flower arrangements were greatly affected by Buddhist culture. Incense was often used to show devotion and respect while chanting, and it was also common practice for the eminent monk to appreciate flowers and burn incense (see figs. 153–154 on pages 122 and 123).

Incense was very popular with the ancient aristocracy. In the traditional mixing of incense, there was a magical product called "Xuanhe royal incense." The raw materials of which were agarwood, *jinyanxiang*, *beiyincao*, borneol, cinnabar, cloves, benzoin, sandalwood, and other incense. It was said that the Emperor Huizong of Song Dynasty used this fragrance, often making it in his own royal incense house, and also giving it to his trusted ministers as a reward.

Most members of the literati were very fond of scents and incense, as reflected in Zhu Xi's writing when he says, "As I look out the window, I sit for a while with incense burning beside me." Wen Zhenheng writes, "The incense burns where windows are bright, tables clean, and the floor swept." Su Shi was a renowned master of fragrance. When appointed as prefect of Hangzhou, he produced a famous incense called "Wensi Incense" (meaning smelling and meditating), made from sandalwood, Chinese figwort, clove, nutgrass galingale rhizome, lakawood, nutmeg, lemon grass, and so forth, with a lingering scent and memory.

CHAPTER 8
BATHING

THE ORIGINAL TEXT

It is always dusty in the capital, and clean windows and tables are always in contact with dust, making them accumulate a thick layer of it over time. Such dusty conditions are brutal for the vase flower arrangements, so they must be washed once a day. Even if a beautiful woman such as Nanwei (the beauty of Jin Kingdom during the Spring and Autumn Period, on par with Xishi) and Qingqin (the celestial fairy from ancient legend) do not put on make-up and comb their hair, it is difficult for them to maintain a charming appearance. In the same way, flowers arranged in a vase are just a smattering of leaves and flowers with a fading fragrance, if they are not maintained properly and are allowed to become contaminated with dust. In such cases, they wither almost immediately, leaving us with nothing left that is worth looking at.

Flowers also have joy and rage, wakefulness and sleep, dawn and nightfall, each in their turn. Bathing is another ritual that should be performed in a timely way for flowers, recalling the rains that moisten it in its natural setting,

Fig. 155 *Flower Book—Chrysanthemum*

Wang Yuan (Yuan Dynasty)
Ink and color on silk
Height 25.9 cm × Width 23.6 cm
Palace Museum, Taibei

Wang Yuan was skilled in painting flowers and birds, and was a leading figure in flower-and-bird paintings during the Yuan Dynasty. The paintings *Hibiscus* (see fig. 156 on page 126) and *Chrysanthemum* in his flower book collection, with a mantis and butterfly enhancing the paintings separately, are exquisitely and elegantly done with rich colors.

when clouds are sparse and the sun is shining, flowers will bloom. In raging winds and on rainy days, or in the scorching sun or bitter cold, flowers will slumber. Just as the red of a woman's lips is reflected in the sunlight, the charming scent of a flower is like a breeze blowing. This is the time of joy, when flowers bloom. When the flower looks drowsy and restrained, whirling like smoke and fog, this is when the flower is worried and exhausted. If the stalk of a flower bends slightly and sinks wearily below the window sill, and the flower looks fragile and weak, it is dreaming. If a flower has a lingering glance, and its brightness dazzles the eyes, this

Fig. 156 *Flower Book—Hibiscus*

is when the bloom is awake and stretching. At dawn, a flower can be placed in an open courtyard or in a grand hall. When it is dark, a flower should be hidden away in an inner room. When it is spent in its sorrow, you should carefully hold your breath. When it is joyful, you too should be joyful, cheering and laughing with it. When it is sleepy and dreary, you should lower the curtain. If the flower awakes, you should dress it up. To do thus is to understand the nature of plants and flowers and respect their rules for living. The best time to wash flowers are when they are in bloom, the second when they sleep, and the least ideal is when they are full of joy. If one washes the flower in the dark of night, when it is worrying, it is like torturing it, and what merit is there in that?

The method for bathing flowers and plants is to carefully pour clean spring waters over them, like a light rain or dew to sober over-drinking or moist hands. The flowers should not be touched with one's hands, nor should fingertips be allowed to scratch them.

One should do the bathing in person rather than get low-brow servants to do it.

The person best equipped to bathe a plum blossom is a hermit in the mountains. The crabapple is best bathed by an elegant, affectionate person. The most suitable person for bathing a peony and herbaceous peony is a gorgeously dressed young girl, while a beautiful maid is best suited for bathing a pomegranate flower. An osmanthus is best washed by a pure and intelligent youth, and a lotus is best bathed by a sweet and charming concubine. A chrysanthemum should be bathed by someone of extraordinary character, and a wintersweet is best washed by an austere monk. In the cold winter season, however, flowers are less resistant to cold water and should instead be cleaned with gossamer. Those who raise flowers should be sympathetic to the style of the flowers, so that their natural beauty may be rejuvenated and their life prolonged; rather than simply making it appear moist and glossy (see fig. 155 on page 125 and fig. 156).

In this section, Yuan Hongdao offers a detailed explanation of the best timing and manner for bathing vase flowers, making a point to note that this elegant, refined work cannot be entrusted to low-brow maids.

1. The Person Bathing the Flowers

Of all flowers, bathing a plum blossom is the most elegant of activities. Poets even had a special term for it, "plum-bath." To bathe a plum blossom, one should be a hermit living in the mountains or forest. In the Northern Song Dynasty, the recluse Lin Bu (967–1029) retired to the lonely mountains of Hangzhou, unmarried and with no children to carry on his line. Instead, he planted plum blossoms and raised cranes, referring to this as his "wife plum blossom and son crane." It was a well-known tradition to use plum blossoms to describe a man of excellent character who had retired into seclusion, so it naturally follows that a hermit would be the most suitable person to bathe a plum blossom.

For bathing a crabapple, the best choice is an elegant person such as Su Shi, who is famously quoted as saying, "Fearful that flowers only sleep in the dead of night, so I burn a tall candle." The crabapple is so radiant and resplendent that he could not bear to leave it alone in the faint darkness. For this reason, it is said that the one who understands the crabapple must be elegant.

The best person to bathe a peony and herbaceous peony is a charming girl, such as the character Du Liniang in the legendary Ming Dynasty play *Peony Pavilion* (*Mudan Ting*), who upon seeing a peony blossoming in her garden can't help but sing, "At first it opened in beautiful purple and brilliant red bloom everywhere, to all relics and remains. Who will enjoy this beautiful view and day? Who will be indulged in such a joyous beauty?"

The pomegranate is best bathed by a beautiful woman, like the pretty girl Chunmei in *The Plum in the Golden Vase*. Chunmei, a very tricky woman, was the most influential figure among the maids. Not only did Ximen Qing dote on her, but after his death she entered the garrison house and at last achieved her ambition and became the wife of the garrison.

The osmanthus should be bathed by a pure, intelligent youth. This is a rough description of the handsome young men like Pan An and Song Yu. When he was young, Pan An was naughty, loving to make mischief with his leather slingshot on the outskirts of the city of Luoyang. When women saw him coming, they would stand hand-in-hand in a circle, surrounding him, throwing fruits to him, hence the term "a full cart loaded with thrown fruits," suggesting the image of "handsome young men."

The lotus should be bathed by a charming woman, such as Li Ping'er in *The Plum in the Golden Vase* or Xiang Ling in *Dream of the Red Mansions* (*Honglou Meng*).

The best person for bathing chrysanthemum is an older man of extraordinary character fond of ancient times, such as Tao Yuanming.

It is best to allow a monk to bathe the wintersweet.

2. Cultural Background

Several cultural items are mentioned in this section.

Bathing and Chinese Culture
Since ancient times, bathing has been associated with the highest types of rituals in Chinese culture. As early as the Shang and

Zhou dynasties, it was stipulated that during major events such as ascending the throne, succession, offerings, a new era, and other major activities, the monarch should fast for three days, bathe and change clothes as a sign of his respect for heaven and earth. This demonstrates that, in the Chinese concept, bathing was not merely for the health of the flesh, but also for the dignity and character of the person (fig. 157).

Nanwei

In the historical record *Strategies of the Warring States* (*Zhanguo Ce*), when Jin Wengong (697–628 BC) received a stunning beauty,

Nanwei, in a certain year, he did not appear in court for three days. Later, he came to his senses and put her away, saying that it was important to be more vigilant and that there must be monarch in the future who would loose his kingdom because he was obsessed with a beautiful woman. This story was passed down as an example of a monarch who consciously—and wisely—removed temptation from before him. Such a story was very much in line with the image of a loyal official. For this reason, though Nanwei does not enjoy an especially good reputation, and though she was not widely known among the ordinary people, the story was relished among the aristocracy.

Maids

Maids were important helpers in the lives of ancient scholars. The gentrified class was quite wealthy, and all their daily needs were attended to by maids. Though Yuan Hongdao was poor, he had no problem keeping a few maids. During the Ming Dynasty, it was not only the gentrified class that kept a number of maids, but also lesser merchants and ordinary citizens. The price of their maids was different, costing roughly two or three silver pieces (currency) for an ordinary servant. The value of a clever maid was four or five pieces of silver, while a talented young maid was worth substantially more.

It was considered quite reasonable to not allow crude people to bathe flowers and vases. The price of a fine vase was from a couple of pieces of silver to a dozen or more. If a common maid shattered a vase, she would never be able to recover the cost of it, even if she were sold to another family.

Fig. 157 *Royal Bath*
Qiu Ying

In this painting, the concubine is like a hibiscus, charming and painted in beautiful colors. Behind her, royal maids hold a flower arrangement, which is fresh and fragrant.

CHAPTER 9
FLOWERS AS FOILS

THE ORIGINAL TEXT

The main flowers are paired with flowers which set them off, just like a harem concubines and maids, and a great lady has maidservants who follow her to her husband's house. Among flowers and plants, there is no lack of glamor. They create fog and rain, and are like the king's favorite. How could they not be included there? Plum blossoms takes winter jasmine, winter daphne, and camellias as maidservants. For the crabapple, apple flower, malus pumila flower, and lilac serve as maidservant. For the peony, the rugosa rose, rose, and Lady Banks' rose serve as maidservant. The herbaceous peony takes poppy, hollyhock as maidservant. For the pomegranate, crape myrtle and Chinese hibiscus serve as maidservant. The lotus takes symplocos and hosta plantaginea as maidservant. The sweet scented osmanthus is served by hibiscus. Chrysanthemum takes yellow or white camellia and the begonia as maidservants. Wintersweet is served by narcissus as its maidservant.

Although the appearance and mood of the maidservants are different from one another, they flourished for a period of time. People have their own judgement and comment on their fluidity and elegance. For instance, the narcissus is aloof and elegant, like the maidservant of weaver girl, Liang Yuqing. The brightly colored camellia is beautiful, the winter daphne has a strong fragrance, the rugosa rose is enchanting, the hibiscus is gorgeous, like the Shi Cong

family's charming maidservant Xuan Feng or the Yang Kan family's dancing girl Zhang Jingwan. The malus pumila flower and apple flower are lovely and elegant like Pan Kang's beloved concubine Zhao Jiechou. Poppies and hollyhock bloom in hedgerows, gorgeous like Luan Tai the maidservant of Sikong Tu. The blooms of the symplocos are pure white and relaxed. They are refined, elegant and graceful, just like Yu Xuanji's maidservant Lü Qiao. The yellow and white camellias win by its charm, just like the maidservant of Guo Wenyuan's family, Chun Feng. The lilac is thin and weak, the hosta plantaginea is poor, and the begonia is sweet and charming, however they have a sense of pedantry of learned people, just like Zheng Xuan and Cui Xiucai's family's servants. Other types of flowers cannot be compared with them. In short, all are renowned around the world. They are gentle and delicate, domineering. And if they are compared to charming women, how could they fail to equal Su Shi's beloved concubine Liu Hua and Bai Juyi's dancer Chun Cao?

On pages 130 and 131

Figs. 158–160 *Flowers of the Four Seasons* (detail)
Shen Zhou
Ink and color on paper
Height 27.5 cm × Width 504.8 cm
The Metropolitan Museum of Art, New York

The traditional literati painting of plum blossoms, orchids, chrysanthemums, and bamboo by Shen Zhou was very diverse and had a far-reaching influence on floriculture painters in later stages.

THE MODERN READER

Flower arrangements were divided into "orders," meaning that certain flowers played the main role, while others acted as their servants. This is the proper use of flowers and plants. In Yuan Hongdao's view, auxiliary floral materials in vase flower arrangements were like charming, beautiful female servants. Bright colored camellia, and daphne are very fragrant, charming and gentle. The rugosa rose and the hibiscus are bright and beautiful. The lilac is thin, and the hosta plantaginea is cold. The begonia is lovely. Each flower is like a beautiful woman, a secluded boudoir of self-pity, pouring out one's grievances and telling a sad, romantic story (figs. 158–160).

Figs. 158–160 *Flowers of the Four Seasons* (detail)

Composition of a Chinese Flower Arrangement

The composition of a traditional Chinese flower arrangement draws on Chinese landscape painting, calligraphy, and traditional Confucian philosophy, giving attention to the posture and charm of a flowering twig. It is modeled with attention to the branch's lines, with a natural, chic aesthetic and a basic spirit is that there is a main and a secondary twig, with attention to juxtaposition and harmony.

The shape of China's traditional flower arrangement takes a main branch as a skeleton, around which the first, second, and third main branches are organized. The main branch is mostly from a ligneous tree, with varying heights and thickness. This is decorated with a variety of herbaceous branches and twigs. The main branch serves as a foil for the other branches, which are situated in clusters to make a full, layered arrangement.

Fig. 161 *Painting to Usher in the New Year* (detail)

Zhao Chang
Ink and color on silk
Height 103.8 cm ×
Width 51.2 cm
Palace Museum, Taibei

The plum blossoms, camellias, narcissus, and other flowers in this picture were painted with cinnabars, titanium white, rouge, and malachite. The colors are bright and beautiful, creating a scene of majestic splendor. The whole painting is filled with lakeside rocks and dense flowers, hardly leaving any empty space. It is neatly and seriously presented, creating a very decorative effect.

1. Flower Pairing

Yuan Hongdao's discussion of the placement of various types of flowers used as primary or secondary subjects in an arrangement reflects the pairings found in Ming and Qing dynasties paintings.

For instance, he says the plum blossom serves as the primary flower, with winter jasmine, daphne, and camellia as maidservant. Plum blossom and camellia are the classic accompaniments in Ming Dynasty flower paintings, all of which bloom after the Spring Festival. The plum blossom is lean and solitary, while the camellia is luxuriant, creating a perfectly complementary pair. If the plum blossom were placed in the vase on its own, it would easily appear cool and thin, but when aligned with the gorgeous camellia, it suddenly becomes festive (fig. 161).

The osmanthus and hibiscus make another classic painting. In the Ming and Qing dynasties flower-and-bird paintings, the osmanthus was often present as the theme in paintings, but the flowers were so small in the image as to be almost indiscernible. The hibiscus is quite different, being a huge, colorful flower. The osmanthus is a sweet, strongly scented flower, while the hibiscus is colorful, but

has no fragrance. This allows the hibiscus to be appropriately paired with the osmanthus (fig. 162).

The wintersweet often appears with the narcissus in Qing Dynasty paintings of decoration for appreciation on the first day of the lunar calendar flower arrangements. The flowering period of both coincides with the Spring Festival, and both were just right for Lunar New Year flower decorations for appreciation. Though the two flowers were harmonious, they were not often arranged together in a single vase. Instead, the

Fig. 162 *Rare Birds in Autumn*
Lü Ji
Ink and color on silk
Height 184 cm × Width 109.5 cm

In this painting, fragrant osmanthus and hibiscus are depicted. The osmanthus is very fragmented, almost indecipherable, with only small bits of golden yellow visible between the leaves. The hibiscus flowers in the distance are huge. The fragrance of the osmanthus spreads far, and the hibiscus flowers bloom beside the water. It is a classic autumn landscape.

Fig. 163
Decoration for Appreciation on the First Day of the Lunar Calendar

Ma Tai (Qing Dynasty)
Ink and color on paper
Height 101 cm × Width 52 cm

This painting depicts wintersweet, and nandina alongside potted pine and narcissus embellished by fingered citron, red candles, firecrackers, and a rabbit. This is a clear depiction of the folk customs of the late Qing Dynasty and Republican period.

wintersweet would be placed in a bottle, with the narcissus used as a bonsai to adorn the side of the vase (fig. 163).

Though some flowers create a very harmonious effect when placed together, and though they flower at the same time, they are rarely used in combination. For instance, the crabapple with apple flower, malus pumila flower, and lilac as foil, was a combination rarely used. Rather it was more common to see the crabapple presented as a foil to the magnolia which served as the main flower in an arrangement.

There were several other unusual pairings mentioned by Yuan Hongdao, such as placing the peony with the rugosa rose, rose, Lady Banks' rose, or herbaceous peony with poppies or hollyhock. The use of pomegranate with crape myrtle or Chinese hibiscus could be considered harmonious, but it was not common. Rather, the pomegranate was more often seen with the calamus or hollyhock. In this section, the lotus is paired with the symplocos and hosta plantaginea, which was rare, with the lotus usually being placed on its own (fig. 164). The chrysanthemum paired with the yellow and white camellia or begonia was also an unusual work.

2. Flowers and Beautiful Women

In order to depict the grace of various flowers, Yuan Hongdao compared them to beautiful women. He mentions well-known maidservants and consorts who were from humble origins but were charismatic. Or they were the beautiful concubines of the rich, powerful, influential officials or were the confidante of a famous literary scholar. The story of Xuan Feng comes from the Jin Dynasty (265–420), depicting the rivalry of the concubines in the house. Zhang Jingwan's slender waist is said to be like water, and she could dance on the palm of the hand as if she were Zhao Feiyan reincarnated. Zhao Jiechou

Fig. 164
Summer Garden

Chen Chun
Ink and color on paper
Height 320.4 cm × Width 99.7 cm
The Metropolitan Museum of Art, New York

This painting is densely filled with flowers, leaves, and jagged rocks of grotesque shapes. The lotus is also not depicted singly, but with its blooms taking up the whole pond, turning it into limpid blue jade. From the poem written by the painter, this painting was created during the hot, humid summer, but a breath of coolness ensues from the painting, momentarily dispersing the sweltering heat.

had great beauty and was a skilled poet. The emperor could not help but show interest in this, and so took forcible possession of this talented, beautiful woman. Unexpectedly, her husband disobeyed the emperor's orders, refusing to hand over the beautiful woman to the monarch.

The maidservant of the Eastern Han Confucian scholar Zheng Xuan (127–200) was familiar with the *Book of Songs*, with words flowing from her mouth as from the pen of a master. Liu Hua, the beloved concubine of Su Shi, and Chun Cao, the dancing girl of the Tang Dynasty poet Bai Juyi (772–846), could all lead to a revival of the literati's reverie in "reading at night with a pretty young woman in his company."

CHAPTER 10
AMATEURISH ATTACHMENT

THE ORIGINAL TEXT

Ji Kang's preference for metalworking, Wu Zi's love of horses, Lu Yu's love for tea, Mi Fu's obsession with strange rocks, and Ni Zan's insistence on cleanliness are all instances of the use of a unique hobby to clear one's pent-up feeling of injustice and express one's elegant talent. In my opinion, people who are dull and unprepossessing are those without a favorite hobby. If a person has a hobby, he will indulge it, devote himself to it wholeheartedly, and plunge his whole life into it. How can such a person still have time to think of money, officiating, or conducting business? People who are fond of flowers always hear of some exotic flower and, no matter how far away or how deep in the valley it is, they will not hesitate to seek it out. The extreme weather of winter and summer cannot deter them. Their skin grows raw and dirty, but they do not care. Wherever the flower blooms, they will lay out their quilt and pillow, camping under the flower so that they can observe its whole process from budding to blooming to dying and falling to the ground. Only then will they leave. Some people observe thousands of flowers in order to thoroughly explore an ever-changing flower. Some appreciate only a part of a particular flower or just a few flowers, finding endless pleasure in that. Some need only sniff the leaf to know the size of a flower, while others need only see the root and stem to determine whether the bloom is red or white. Only such individuals can be said to truly love and enjoy flowers. If I speak of growing flowers, I speak only of passing times of idleness and my loneliness and solitude. I do not truly love flowers. If I really loved them, I would have already become a hermit in the Peach Blossom Orchard—how could I continue serving as a petty official in the secular world?

Fig. 165 *Fallen Flowers* (detail)
Shen Zhou
Ink and dark green color on silk
Height 30.7 cm × Width 138.6 cm
Palace Museum, Taibei

In this painting, a scholar sits alone in the woods overlooking the mountain on the other side. The forest and flowers are fading. It is a colorful image, with petals falling all over the ground. Appreciating fallen flowers in a retreat, the artist expresses his desire to draw refinement out of the dust. The painting is stylistically elegant, loaded with meaning.

THE MODERN READER

Yuan Hongdao believed that the love of something should be extreme and frenzied (figs. 165–166), defining love as a sort of addiction or obsession that would drive one to disregard everything else in life. To this end, he mentions five celebrated figures.

Ji Kang (223–262 or 224–263), during Wei and Jin dynasties, was known as a wild individual who was one of the "Seven Sages of the Bamboo Grove." He hid in the bamboo forest, keeping aloof from the world. In his back yard, beneath a willow tree with dense foliage, he diverted a mountain spring and built a pool by the willow tree. When he was tired from working with metal, he went into the pool and soaked. He used metalworking to express his withdrawal from and contempt for the world.

Wu Zi is the pseudonym for the Jin Dynasty figure Wang Ji. Wang was brilliant, graceful, and heroic. When his period of service was over, he was the officer to the valiant calvary general. Wang loved archery and horses, and was very brave. He lived quite extravagantly and was conferred the title of *Piaoqi* General.

Lu Yu (733–c. 804) was from the Tang Dynasty town of Jingling (now Tianmen, Hubei Province). He was an expert on

Fig. 166 *Landscape and Figures III* (detail)
Chen Hongshou
Ink and color on paper
Height 33.4 cm × Width 27.3 cm
Freer Gallery of Art, Washington D.C.

In late autumn, when the weather is bleak, a nobleman walks, with the aid of his staff, creating an air of being left alone in the world. Behind him stands a tall tree, its red leaves falling into the streams among the drifts.

tea ceremonies, and penned the first ever monograph on tea, called *The Tea Classic (Cha Jing)*. Lu Yu was known as the Tea God.

Mi Fu, a Northern Song Dynasty calligrapher and painter, was a bizarre, eccentric man. He was known as Mi Dian or Mi Chi. He loved to arrange strange rockeries in various places, a hobby with which he was quite obsessed. According to the records, when he was an official in Wuwei County of Anhui

Fig. 167 *Mi Fu Worshipping the Stone* (detail)
Chen Hongshou
Ink and color on silk
Height 112 cm × Width 50 cm

Mi Fu made a hobby of appreciating stones. It was said that upon seeing one particularly strange stone, he grew ecstatic, then knelt before it and made obeisance over and over. In this painting, Mi Fu looks enamored and fascinated, reveling his scholarly nobility and admiration for the ancient.

Province, he heard there was a strange stone, one which the locals regarded as an immortal stone, and so did not dare tamper with it. Mi Fu sent people to move it to his own residence, setting up a ritual table. Offerings were made to the rock, and it was called by later generations "Mi Fu worshipping stone" (fig. 167).

Ni Zan (1306 or 1301–1374) was a Yuan Dynasty painter. Alongside Huang Gongwang (1269–1354), Wu Zhen (1280–1354), and Wang Meng, he was known as one of the "Four Yuan Scholars." As a landscape painter, he had a simple, detached style. Ni Zan's temperament was lofty and aloof, and he was obsessed with cleanliness. He wore a cloak and peasant's hat that had to be cleaned thousands of times. He even ordered the servants to wash the phoenix tree and rockery outside his study several times a day. It was said the phoenix tree grew so depressed with this procedure it could not bear leaves anymore and eventually died. If a guest came to visit, as soon as he departed, Ni Zan had the seat he had sat in swept. Once, when a guest stayed in his house, he heard coughing in a neighboring room during the night. The next morning, he ordered a servant to search carefully for traces of phlegm. When the servant could find none, the hypothesis was given that perhaps the one coughing had spit onto the leaves of the phoenix tree outside the window. Ni Zan ordered that the leaves be cut from the tree and discarded at some distance from his residence.

These were so called "true celebrities with real style." Celebrated figures are naturally unique. The good side of this is that they have a particular style to their personalities. The bad side is that this style can become a defect. It is for this reason that Yuan Hongdao laments, "People who are

dull and unprepossessing are all drab in language and repulsive in appearance." A person who does not have a strong suit, who lives flatly, speaks ignorantly, and has nothing of value to say, is truly dull.

On page 139

Fig. 168 *Five Representatives of Pureness* (detail)
Yun Shouping
Ink on silk
Height 86.1 cm × Width 38.4 cm
Palace Museum, Taibei

In the top part of the painting, the branches of an old pine tree traverse from right to left, while the clear moon hangs high in the sky. The middle portion of the painting has blooming plum blossoms accompanying green bamboo. A gurgling stream occupies the bottom part of the picture, completing it. Using plum blossoms, pine, bamboo, water, and moon to signify "pureness," the painting expresses the lofty and non-vulgar sentiment of a gentleman.

CHAPTER 11
APPRECIATION

THE ORIGINAL TEXT

Drinking tea while appreciating flowers is the most elegant. Next is to discuss with each other when viewing flowers, and drinking wine while appreciating flowers is the worst. Drinking wine made from the court's workshops or tea from the State of Yue, or using filthy or vulgar language, displeases the spirit of the flowers. Those who appreciate flowers would prefer to sit to one side, mouths tightly shut and not uttering a word, rather than offend the flowers. Flowers must be viewed at the right time and place, so it is insulting to invite guests casually. The appreciation of winter flowers is most suitable during an early snowfall, on a sunny day after the snow, or in a warm room, or under the new moon. Spring flowers are best enjoyed on a sunny day, or when the weather is cold, or in an elegant hall. Enjoyment of summer flowers is best after a new rain, or in a breeze, or in the shade of a nice tree, beneath bamboo, or in a pavilion by the water. Autumn flowers are best enjoyed on a cool moonlight night, at sunset, on a spacious flight of steps, or on a mossy roadside embankment, or beside the old vine and the mountain rocks. If we ignore the weather conditions and fail to choose a suitable place, the spirit of the flower will grow dull, putting it completely out of harmony with its environment. How would that be any different from viewing flowers in a brothel?

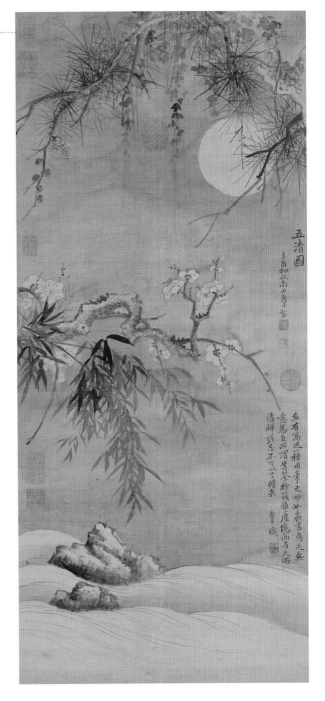

The elegant taste and aesthetic characteristic of flower appreciation not only gave attention to time and nature's goodness, but also to the environment and the flower's placement within it, so as to highlight the flowers and their character, in the pursuit of refined, elegant taste (see fig. 168 on page 139).

1. How to Appreciate Flowers

The appreciation of flowers is accompanied by tea, discussion, wine, music, fragrance, and instrument, among other things. Of these, Tang Dynasty wine tasting and music appreciation, late Tang and Five Dynasties fragrance appreciation, Song Dynasty musical instrument appreciation, and Ming Dynasty appreciation of tea were highly specialized fields.

Wine appreciation. The Tang Dynasty was a time of warm enthusiasm, bold passion, and luxurious splendor. Wine and flower appreciation were widespread among the nobility during this time, with crowds gathering to drink wine and compose poetry or paint, making for great literary and flower appreciation events. In *Preface to Peach and Plum Garden at a Spring Night Banquet*, Li Bai wrote that in the season of fragrant blossoms of peaches and plums, he and his companions feasted and drank together beneath the willows in a misty garden, viewing the night flowers, drinking wine and composing poetry. Leng Mei's *Banquet in the Peach Orchard on a Spring Night* depicts this scene (fig. 169). It was not the style of the Tang Dynasty for each person to sit idly and drink only a single cup of tea.

Music appreciation. The Tang Dynasty also excelled in music appreciation, which is to say, viewing flowers while listening to music. The three verses of Li Bai's poem from *Qingpingdiao* were written in appreciation of the peony. On a spring day in the first year of the Tianbao reign (742–756), the Tang Emperor Xuanzong and Concubine Yang viewed peonies at the palace of Chenxiang Pavilion, summoning Li Bai to the palace to record the event. One of the verses includes the lines, "The renowned flower and the beautiful concubine bring a smile to kings' faces." He wrote in a style full of pomp and richness about the unsurpassed beauty Concubine Yang being favored. Greatly pleased, the emperor immediately ordered the performers in the operatic circle to compose a tune, play a musical instrument, and had the song promptly performed by Li Guinian.

Aroma appreciation. During the late Tang and the Five Dynasties, incense was burned when the flowers were in bloom. Han Xizai particularly favored this practice, allowing the natural fragrance of the flowers to mingle with the aroma of the incense, having a great effect on the development of flower arrangement.

Musical instrument appreciation. The literati during the Song Dynasty advocated elegance and taste, initiating musical instrument appreciation. The appreciation of elegant, fragrant flowers was complemented with instruments such as the zither and lute,

Fig. 169 *Banquet in the Peach Orchard on a Spring Night*
Leng Mei (Qing Dynasty)
Ink and color on silk
Height 188.4 cm × Width 95.6 cm
Palace Museum, Taibei

Appreciating flowers at a feast and composing poetry were activities that summed up the elegant life of officials. In this painting, the blossoming courtyards are brightly lit, and the moon shines overhead. A few scholars drink wine around stone tables, with several servants at their side.

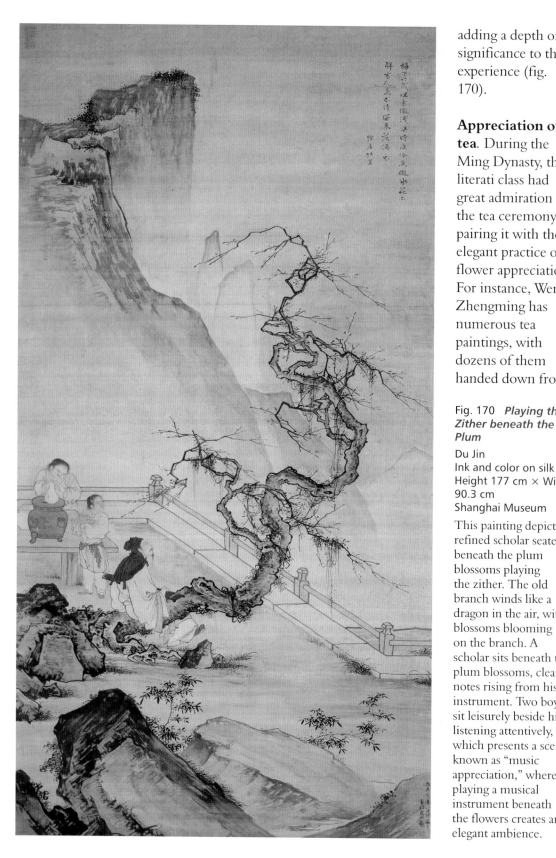

adding a depth of significance to the experience (fig. 170).

Appreciation of tea. During the Ming Dynasty, the literati class had great admiration for the tea ceremony, pairing it with the elegant practice of flower appreciation. For instance, Wen Zhengming has numerous tea paintings, with dozens of them handed down from

Fig. 170 *Playing the Zither beneath the Plum*
Du Jin
Ink and color on silk
Height 177 cm × Width 90.3 cm
Shanghai Museum

This painting depicts a refined scholar seated beneath the plum blossoms playing the zither. The old branch winds like a dragon in the air, with blossoms blooming on the branch. A scholar sits beneath the plum blossoms, clear notes rising from his instrument. Two boys sit leisurely beside him, listening attentively, which presents a scene known as "music appreciation," where playing a musical instrument beneath the flowers creates an elegant ambience.

one generation to another, including *Tea Gathering in Huishan* (see fig. 122 on page 87), demonstrating how popular the tea ceremony was. By this time, it was considered quite gauche to drink wine beneath a flowering tree, as had been done in the Tang Dynasty.

2. Choosing a Time for Flower Appreciation

Regardless how one went about appreciating flowers, choosing the appropriate and the correct time of day was important. The ancients often discussed proper timing, beautiful scenery, pleasing sensibilities, and joyous things, believing that the combination of these four considerations was one of life's great blessings.

Yuan Hongdao believed that it was most appropriate to view winter flowers during the first snow, on the sunny day after snow, or during the new moon. When snow was falling, it was the perfect time to admire plum blossoms. After a snowfall, the plum blossom appeared cold and solitary. On the night of the new moon, viewing the plum blossom alone gave one a greater feeling of "burying withered flowers under the cold lonely moon." In spring, flowers were best appreciated on sunny but cold days. The scenery in the spring was clear, and when the weather was fine, the apricot blossoms were quite picturesque (fig. 171) and the peach blossoms were intoxicating. In a light, cold mist, the view was even more interesting. In summer, flower appreciation was best on rainy or windy days. After a new rain or in a cool breeze, the lotus bloomed in the lotus pond, its leaves clear like water and the flowers tender and beautiful as if reflecting the day, inexplicably beautiful. In autumn, it was best to appreciate flowers on a moonlit night or at sunset. The sweet-scented osmanthus was particularly fragrant in mid-autumn under a bright moon. The hibiscus, when reflected in the water looked

Fig. 171 *Sketches of Apricot* (detail)
Zhao Chang
Ink and color on silk
Height 25.2 cm × Width 27.3 cm
Palace Museum, Taibei

This painting depicts only a branch of apricot blossom. The exuberant flowers display an enriching sense of spring. The ink is delicate and exquisite.

like colored clouds fallen from the sky.

Only in certain circumstances and at certain times of day could one see flowers at their best.

3. The Environment for Flower Appreciation

It is necessary to give attention to the environment and placement of the flowers. In the Ming Dynasty, flower appreciation often took place in a garden. The garden landscape with elements such as rockeries, waters, plants, architecture, and birds and animals were all carefully arranged in such a way as to set off the flowers, giving it all the elegance and charm of flower appreciation. In summer the shade from trees, a green bamboo grove, or an exquisite water pavilion was the best place from which to view flowers. In autumn, the most suitable spots were on steps, mossy paths or an embankment of ancient stone. Canal sides, beside small bridges, next to bamboo or pine, and bright windows and clear hedgerows were all places in which the scenery was suited to the setting of flower arrangements.

Fig. 172 *Narcissi and Wintersweet*
Qiu Ying
Ink and color on silk
Height 47.5 cm × Wdith 25 cm
Palace Museum, Taibei

The painting depicts the harsh winter season, with two stalks of narcissus standing together, while a stalk of wintersweet sails lightly into the picture from the top, reflecting a beautiful concept. The artist's exquisite brushwork gave full expression to the fresh and elegant poise and charm of the two types of fragrant flowers.

CHAPTER 12
SUPERVISION

THE ORIGINAL TEXT

Taste of Plum (*Mei Pin*) was quite lovingly written by the Song Dynasty writer Zhang Gongfu. After reading it, I admired it greatly, and have imitated it in parts to include in my study of vase flower arrangements.

There are fourteen things that are pleasing for vase flower arrangements: a bright window; clean shelves; ancient bronze tripods; famous inkstones from the Song Dynasty; whistling of the wind in the pines; water in the brook; a passionate master who is a skilled poet; a household monk (for exalted households to conduct rituals, staying in constant contact) who knows how to brew tea; people from Jizhou (a wine-producing region in Northern Tianjin that was renowned since ancient times and was especially popular in the Ming and Qing dynasties) bringing wine; guests seated were skilled in painting flowers; good friends came to visit just when the flowers were blooming; copied books on growing flowers with my own hand; a kettle whistling on the stove late at night; and a virtuous wife and a beautiful maidservant by which to verify the allusions related to flowers.

There are twenty-three things that are offensive to flowers: an owner keen to entertain frequent visitors; vulgar people mixed in with people appreciating flowers; an artificially bent twig; untrained monks ranting about the teachings of Zen beneath the flowers; dogs fighting beneath the window; inviting singing children from the Lotus Lane to sing; Yiyang style opera is sung during the banquet (one of the popular opera singing styles of the Ming Dynasty); an ugly woman wearing a flower in her hair; talking about official promotions while viewing flowers; pretending to love flowers one is not fond of; writing poetry endlessly for various occasions; families forcing one to settle accounts while the flowers are blooming; checking characters from the book *On Rhyming* (*Yun Fu*) for rhymes when writing poems; the shameful sight of damaged or messy books; intermediaries from Fujian doing business to promote sales; fake paintings from Suzhou; mouse faeces under the flowers; snails crawling among the flowers' stems; arrogant or rude maids; running out of wine as soon as one has started drinking; the places to view flowers attached to a noisy wine house; cliche's like "purple aura in central plains" or "golden and snow white" placed on the table; and the atmosphere of entertainment that is particularly popular in Beijing, where people set up red screens and enjoy a modest reward every time a flower blooms. In my opinion, such people actually insult flowers. There are, in fact, few people who truly understand flowers. Humble hearts check their own behavior, and because people often make mistakes that insult flowers, I write the above as a reminder to myself (fig. 172).

Flower appreciation requires the proper timing and weather, as well as the setting and accompaniments. It also manifests the character of both the flowers and the one appreciating them and pursues the elegance detached from worldly taste. For the joy in the beauty and character of the flower, the person, the main body of flower appreciation, should acquire refined taste (fig. 173).

1. Pleasing Practices

Taste of Plum was written by the Southern Song Dynasty official Zhang Gongfu in 1194, in which he specifically introduces how one might admire the plum blossom. The work was included in *Mundane Remarks (Qidong Yeyu)*, a well-written note by Zhou Mi, a famous scholar of the late Song, early Yuan Dynasty. It is 600 characters in length. The author wrote in his preface that he had purchased a derelict garden on the shores of South Lake and meticulously transferred it into a plum garden, attracting endless streams of guests to admire the plum blossoms. However, many of the visitors missed the point, being empty-minded, leaving him no choice but to list out the basic criterion for viewing plum blossoms and post in the hall of the plum garden. There are fifty articles in *Taste of Plum*, including "Flower Propriety," "What Flower Are Jealousy of," "Flower in Good Grace," and "Flower Humiliation." Zheng Gongfu believed that the people most suited to engage in activities surrounding the plum blossom were pipers in the forest, musical instrument players, chess players on a stone plate, tea-makers making tea in snow, and beautiful women in light makeup.

Inspired by *Taste of Plum*, Yuan Hongdao listed the elegant activities pleasing for flower appreciation. The idea was to grasp and perceive some sort of personality or spirit advocated by the aesthetic subject from the natural features of the object, such as the color and fragrance of flowers, like the noble spirit of the plum blossom, the high standards of the chrysanthemum, or the elegance of the lotus. Appreciation of these qualities required meditation on the object.

2. Insulting the Flowers

Yuan Hondao lists twenty-three activities that were insulting to flowers. In so doing, he was not so much writing about flowers as he was making a social record of the Ming Dynasty.

The prominence of homosexuality in Ming Dynasty circles was a manifestation of the celebrities savvy, free-spirited nature. The text mentions the songs of children in the Lotus Lane, referring to the young child in the tavern that sing in order to sell oneself, as the Lotus Lane was the gathering place for these young singers at that time. Yuan thought inviting the singers from Lotus Lane to appreciate flowers were an offensive sight.

In the same way, during the flower-viewing season, businessmen from Fujian or fake paintings produced in Suzhou of the famous Wuzhong masters such as Tang Yin, Wen Zhengming, or others, as well as cliches like "purple aura in central plains" or "golden and snow white" are all similar cases. Each of these examples makes him feel uncomfortable.

From the Wanli period of the Ming Dynasty to the middle of the Qing Dynasty, a group of master folk painters gathered in Shantang Street, Zhuanzhu Alley and the Taohuawu area in Suzhou. The fake paintings were created exclusively for the industry, and the fake paintings were collectively referred

Fig. 173 *Landscape and Figures VI* (detail)

Chen Hongshou
Ink and color on paper
Height 33.4 cm ×
Width 27.3 cm
Freer Gallery of Art,
Washington D.C.

The main attraction in this painting is the landscape. In the boat depicted in the painting, two scholars sit, talking. An empty vase is in the boat, ready to hold flowers.

leading voices in the Jiangnan literary world during the Ming Dynasty. Wang's influence in Wuzhong was particularly far-reaching. What Yuan Hongdao finds disappointing is not the saying, but Wang himself. Wang's retro style had a large number of imitators. The malpractice of this genre was that later followers often uttered the motto, commonly using lines from poetry, such as "golden, snow white" or "purple aura in central plains." Yuan was very disgusted with this practice, believing it should be changed with times to preserve what is real and true, and to express feelings and emotions from deep down.

to as "Suzhou Pieces." The materials used in "Suzhou Pieces" were fine silk produced in Huqiu, Shantang, and other places in Suzhou. They were mostly forgeries of Tang, Song, and Ming dynasties masterpieces, the themes of which were mainly green landscape and figure painting. The paintings were copies of works by such famous artists as Shen Zhou, Qiu Ying, Wen Zhengming, and Tang Yin of the Wumen School. Many are still in circulation today. These paintings flowed into the capital in large numbers, the finest of them even making their way into the palace collection.

"Purple aura in central plains" was a favorite phrase of Wang Shizhen, one of the

All in all, *History of Vases* not only concerns itself with flower arrangement, but also offers a personal record of Yuan Hongdao himself, demonstrating his good character and his literary views, and even offering some insight into Ming Dynasty affairs.

APPENDICES

Dates of the Chinese Dynasties

Xia Dynasty（夏）..2100–1600 BC

Shang Dynasty（商）...1600–1046 BC

Zhou Dynasty（周）..1046–256 BC

    Western Zhou Dynasty（西周）.......................................1046–771 BC

    Eastern Zhou Dynasty（东周）..770–256 BC

        Spring and Autumn Period（春秋）..........................770–476 BC

        Warring States Period（战国）...............................475–221 BC

Qin Dynasty（秦）..221–206 BC

Han Dynasty（汉）...206 BC–AD 220

    Western Han Dynasty（西汉）...206 BC–AD 25

    Eastern Han Dynasty（东汉）..25–220

Three Kingdoms（三国）...220–280

    Wei（魏）..220–265

    Shu Han（蜀）..221–263

    Wu（吴）..222–280

Jin Dynasty（晋）..265–420

    Western Jin Dynasty（西晋）..265–316

    Eastern Jin Dynasty（东晋）..317–420

Northern and Southern Dynasties（南北朝）..............................420–589

    Southern Dynasties（南朝）...420–589

    Liang Dynasty（梁）...502–557

    Northern Dynasties（北朝）...439–581

Sui Dynasty（隋）...581–618

Tang Dynasty（唐）...618–907

Five Dynasties and Ten Kingdoms（五代十国）...........................907–960

    Five Dynasties（五代）...907–960

    Ten Kingdoms（十国）..902–979

Song Dynasty（宋）...960–1279

    Northern Song Dynasty（北宋）......................................960–1127

    Southern Song Dynasty（南宋）......................................1127–1279

Liao Dynasty（辽）..916–1125

Jin Dynasty（金）...1115–1234

Xixia Dynasty (or Tangut)（西夏）...1038–1227

Yuan Dynasty（元）...1279–1368

Ming Dynasty（明）...1368–1644

Qing Dynasty（清）...1644–1911

Index